Happy Birthday
with love Sard
on your 17+
xx
Diana

CW00852988

First published in Great Britain in 2018

Copyright © 2018 Jane Bradley
Contact – jane@tgsb.co.uk

Jane Bradley has asserted her moral right to be identified as the Author of this Work in accordance with the Copyright Designs and Patents Act 1988.

All rights reserved. No part of this publication may be reproduced, stored in or introduced into a retrieval system, or transmitted, in any form, or by any means (electronic, mechanical, photocopying, recording or otherwise) without the prior written permission of the author. Any person who does any unauthorised act in relation to this publication or manuscript may be liable to criminal prosecution and civil claims damages.

Matador
9 Priory Business Park,
Wistow Road, Kibworth Beauchamp,
Leicestershire. LE8 0RX
Tel: 0116 279 2299
Email: books@troubador.co.uk
Web: www.troubador.co.uk/matador
Twitter: @matadorbooks

ISBN 978 1789014 464

British Library Cataloguing in Publication Data.
A catalogue record for this book is available from the British Library.

Printed and bound by CPI Group (UK) Ltd, Croydon, CR0 4YY

Matador is an imprint of Troubador Publishing Ltd

Ilustrations – Ian McDermott (ianmcdermott.co.uk)
Book design – Graeme White (graeme@alfol.co.uk)
copyright © Jane Bradley.

www.TGSB.co.uk @thetgsb Teenage Girls Survival Bible @theTGSB

THIS BOOK IS DEDICATED

to my mum, my dad, and to all my dearest friends for being (collectively) the sister I never had. I love you all!

"It takes the teenager back to basics with a truly open and encouraging tone and offers honest and totally achievable advice about self-perception, giving the power back to you. I would recommend this book to any teenage girl"

MARY MCCARTNEY –
Photographer and Vegetarian Cookery Writer

*"If you're a teenager buying this, you and your friends will devour it's pages and probably **read it to death**."*

GEORGIA BYNG –
New York Times Best Selling Children's Author

*"This Survival Bible is what we all wish we had growing up! It's the **must have guide to give for every teen girl** in your life"*

LEONA LEWIS –
Singer and Actress

"It answers many questions that might be difficult or awkward to ask out loud"

VICTORIA PENDLETON, CBE –
Gold-medal winning Olympian

4

INTRODUCTION

(or, what on earth this book is all about and who the heck I am telling you what to do!)

WOULDN'T IT BE GREAT to sail through your teenage years without putting a single foot wrong! Nice idea? Yeah; good luck with that! But how about surviving your teenage years putting the odd foot wrong, but not half as many times as you would have had you not read this book? Yes? Well good - then you've come to the right place; the Teenage Girls Survival Bible. Damn, I wish someone had written this for me when I needed it!

You see, sometimes it's embarrassing talking to your parents about some things isn't it, especially if you've only got one and it happens to be a member of the opposite sex (going bra shopping with your dad or discussing tampons isn't exactly ideal, is it.) What if your mum gets embarrassed easily and doesn't know how to broach certain subjects, or what if your parents are waiting for you to ask about 'grown up things', believing that you'll 'ask when you're ready'? Half the time these important conversations are never had (for all sorts of reasons) and maybe they haven't even thought of half the things you'll learn about in this book, and even if they have, it's possible they think you're either too young to know, too sweet and innocent to need to know, or they're just hoping you'll either learn about it at school or you'll just work it out the hard way (like they did)!

Being a teenage girl is tough. Your hormones go into overdrive and your body and your mind start taking on a whole new unfamiliar shape. A minefield of decisions and choices lie ahead which you'll somehow have to navigate and, somehow, come out the other side intact. While it may not be easy, it's going to be interesting and hopefully, with a big dose of my advice, you'll breeze through this exciting but confusing period of your life.

CONTENTS

ALL ABOUT ME!

I SUPPOSE if we're going to talk intimately about things we should become acquainted first and I should tell you a bit about myself....and why on earth you should listen to anything I've got to say!!!

I don't have children....so I don't have teenagers! Oh hangonaminute.... yes I do....not my own, but I DO have two fantastic teenage girls in my life who I absolutely adore (thanks to my amazing boyfriend and Superdad) and it's precisely because of these two that I decided to write this book.

LET'S GO BACK A BIT FIRST.
When I was a little girl I was extremely shy (hard to believe now; I'm such a show off!!). I thought I was ugly; I didn't like how I looked and was bullied....and as a typically sensitive Virgo I found this crushing. I reached puberty and my ears stuck out (or so I thought) I was goofy (teeth like broken glass) and lanky (a human runner bean with limbs) – it wasn't pretty. Fortunately for me my mother was aware of my self-loathing and made it her business to instil self-love, self-belief and self-confidence into me....a hard task....but it worked....eventually. I cannot IMAGINE how my life would have panned out without such an incredible role model guiding me through the obstacles of growing up. Thankfully, in time my face and my body all started to fall into place and the Ugly Duckling period passed, and when I was 23 I decided to follow my ambition of becoming a make-up artist. I moved from Yorkshire to London where, pretty much, my dreams came true, and over the last 25 years I've travelled all over the world making up everyone from models to rock stars to royalty. Not bad for that self-doubting insecure shy girl is it; I didn't see that coming!!

As much as my daily life constantly changes there's one thing, one factor, which always stays the same....and that's the age of the models I work with; I've basically spent years in the company of teenage girls and I tell you, I've heard it all. I must have heard every bit of teenage girl angst in the book and, I think because of my experiences growing up, I've been able to offer some pretty sound advice (apparently I'm good at it....but you can be the judge of that!). I get on brilliantly with girls and have lots of very close girlfriends....enough to provide seven god children; five of which girls who are nearly all teenagers now, and I love nothing more than spending time in their company and watching and helping them grow.

SO, how about you think of me as a big sister; the one that doesn't steal your makeup or yell at you for being annoying....or runs off to your parents and tells them everything you've been up to and drops you right in it. I'm here to help fill in the gaps and help you make the right choices about LOTS of things and explain some of the more personal sides to being a woman. I'm going to help you to look good, feel good and let you in on a few secrets about boys. You'll learn how to go out without coming to any harm, have sex without getting pregnant or catching horrid diseases, and get your own way without upsetting anyone. We'll talk about love and heartbreak, bitches and bullies, drugs and alcohol. In short (or long!).... everything you need to know but are too afraid to ask!

Photo:marymccartney.com

9

IT'S ALL ABOUT
Survival

GOING OUT

IF YOU'RE AT that age when you're able to go out to bars and parties you're definitely going to need to need to read this.....especially if you want your parents to allow you to go out without having a complete meltdown. Obviously your No1 mission is to have a bloody brilliant time but your parents (the one's making the decisions no doubt) have a different objective altogether. While they want you to have a 'brilliant time' their No1 priority is that you do so safely, and that you get home unharmed. Hardly unreasonable is it. What you need to do is show them that you've thought it all through and that you're heading out the door with a whole host of 'life preserving' tips.

BEING STREETWISE

THERE ARE SOME THINGS YOU SHOULD NEVER LEAVE THE HOUSE WITHOUT:

✓ House keys. Never leave home without your keys but perhaps separate them from other important keys so that IF you lost them it would at least be just those.

✓ Your phone....fully charged.

✓ Money and 'Emergency money'. Emergency money is enough money to get you home in a taxi (should a disaster strike) which you can hide in a separate bit of your purse which you promise yourself you won't spend. Pretend it's not there. Money? What money? You could maybe borrow it from your folks and give it back the next day. This will give them peace of mind that you're not going to get stranded somewhere.

✓ Your parents phone number written down which can live with the Emergency Money. If you get your phone stolen or you drop it down the toilet for instance you could well forget your home number in the ensuing confusion....especially if you've drank too much (which is why you probably lost your phone in the first place!!) At least you'll have a number AND some cash.

✓ Make sure you don't have anything with your home address written on it....in your bag....along with the aforementioned House Keys. Imagine.... you get your bag stolen (well you're not concentrating because you're having such a grrrreat time aren't you) and the thief not only nicks your money and throws away your fav bag (and fab new lipstick) he then hot foots it round to your place (knowing you're out), lets himself in and bingo – he's having a field day! Believe it or not this kind of thing actually happens and often in broad daylight!

✓ If you look young for your age and regularly get asked for I.D. why not do what Tilly does. She photographs her passport and has it to hand on her phone to prove how old she is.....without taking the actual passport which she will inevitably lose.

So, armed to the hilt off you go. Now while most people are pretty decent and, like you, are just out to have a good time, there are those who have more sinister things on their minds. While it's unlikely anything bad will happen to you, you need to be 'streetwise'. Being streetwise gets you home safe and lets others know you're not a pushover. So, here's how to be Streetwise:

For simple starters, how about wearing a 'cross body' bag? Something small and cool which you'll never have to worry about putting down (and getting stolen) even when you're dancing. Buy one with a zipper. (great for festivals!)

Never leave your drink unattended at a bar or at a party. If a boy spiked your drink (dropped drugs into it while you weren't looking) you wouldn't know until it was too late. The warning signs to watch out for include feeling light-headed, sleepy, disorientated or sick; especially if you've had little or no alcohol. You may struggle to stand or walk too which is precisely when the culprit makes his move, and kindly offers to escort you outside 'for some air'. Never EVER ever trust a stranger in this situation. If your friends aren't nearby, ask the bar person for help and say 'I think I've had my drink spiked'. Sadly, I know someone this happened to and with devastating consequences. THINK when you drink. Be AWARE. Never accept a drink off a boy unless you see it poured at the bar.

Never ever presume just because a boy's handsome or seems nice that he's automatically as lovely as you think; you can never tell when you meet a stranger. If he asks you to go somewhere else, just the two of you, tell him you just need to tell your friends and give them his number or better still take a 'fun' picture of the two of you and text it to your friends. If he tells you you're being silly or gets funny about it....don't go. If you DO go back to his house or his friend's house TEXT THE ADDRESS to your parents or at least your friends. Never feel foolish for doing this – it tells him you're strong and intelligent and if anything, if he's nice, he'll really respect you for your self-respect. You're being strong, safe and Streetwise. These measures could save your life.

Make a pact with your friends to leave together or at least at the end of the evening make sure you've all taken the measures above to help keep each of you safe.

Never ever EVER get into an unlicensed minicab or a car claiming to be one. ALWAYS pre-book, use an App or at least phone a trusted registered taxi company, even if it means waiting a bit. My boyfriend's daughter, Issy, told me if ever she gets into a minicab late at night on her own she makes a point of taking a photo of the car registration plate. She texts it to her dad then apologises to the driver and says 'sorry, my dad always makes me do it' and pretends to be embarrassed. She came up with this clever idea herself which I simply had to share with you. She epitomizes the word 'Streetwise' which is brilliant.

♥ If you live only a short walk home and it's dark, always carry your phone in your hand. If you see someone who makes you feel a bit nervous, cross over the road. Usually they're just people trying to get home like you, but if they still give you a creepy feeling pretend to ring home and say in a cheery voice 'hi Dad it's me....I'm almost outside, can you see me from the window?'....then maybe wave to your imaginary father. If a 'would be' attacker thought for a second he'd been seen he'd do an about turn and leg it pretty pronto.

♥ As above, have your keys in your hand to avoid rummaging through your handbag at the front door so you can get inside straight away. I always check behind me when I come home late (it's just habit now) to make sure nobody's lurking behind the hedge! Talking of which....if I get home late at night and have to park my car on another street I always walk on the actual road (I live on a quiet street!) and not close to any sheltered gateways or driveways....if anyone was thinking about pouncing out at least I'd have a head start.

> "It could have cost us our lives"

♥ Never EVER....EV-ERRRRRR get into a car if you know the driver has been drinking or taking drugs. If you suspect the driver is even a bit drunk or a bit high, don't get in the car. Many years ago when I lived in Hong Kong I went out to a party with my then boyfriend. He insisted on driving us home afterwards and even though I knew he'd been drinking I got in the car as he assured me he was 'fine to drive'. What a fool. I'd been drinking too so I wasn't thinking straight and if I'm honest didn't want to make a fuss, but sure enough he fell asleep at the wheel and wrote off his very nice sports car. Fortunately, we were both absolutely fine – saved by a crash barrier at the foot of a high overpass we were about to drive on. I shudder to think of the outcome had he fallen asleep just a few seconds later; it could have cost us our lives. Gives me the shivers!!!

♥ Don't think that because it's daylight nothing bad will happen. I must stress that bad things happen very rarely but it's always good to be alert. Stick to routes which are busy and avoid quiet short cuts ESPECIALLY at night – it's just not worth the risk. If you ever feel uncomfortable about someone either coming towards you or behind you....just leg it. It doesn't matter what the stranger thinks of you; if he thinks you're a madwoman who cares? You'll never see him again. Never think you have to 'style it out'; just put one leg in front of the other and run like the clappers (no, I don't know what clappers are but presumably, they're fast!!)

♥ If you're in a secluded place like a country lane or pathway never ever stop to talk to a stranger. If a man stops to ask you the time for instance just keep walking....or leg it, again. Just run.

♥ Sometimes things can happen in busy places such as public transport; these are usually chancers who try to cop a cheeky feel. If this happens to you, say out loud 'what are you doing' or 'get your hands off' so that everybody nearby can hear. Guaranteed he'll get off at the next stop!

I hope I'm not freaking you out; the world isn't a bad place and there are millions of wonderful harmless people in it (and thousands of good times to be had) but you just need to be aware that it's also not Disneyland either. S**t happens so just make sure it doesn't happen to you.

STAYING IN

THE DARKER SIDE OF SURFING THE NET.

BEING CYBERWISE – LOOKING FOR ANSWERS ONLINE

It's all well and good being streetwise but there's somewhere else you need to stay safe....and that's right there at home. If, like a typical teenager, you like to hole yourself up in your room at night and have a scout around the Internet, you need to be on your guard. It's a source of so much brilliant information but it's also a place where some rather dubious characters can lurk, and they love nothing more than a young vulnerable mind to infect with their poisonous ideas or intentions. I'm talking about Chat Rooms!

I know it's not always easy discussing your problems with your parents or friends, and I can see why you might look for answers online, but please don't blindly trust what these strangers have to say. While your friends may be able to help (they might even secretly share the same concerns as you) your parents or other family members might just surprise you too. Older people have been through more; they've lived longer and have more life experience which automatically makes them a good choice of confidante. However, one person isn't always as kind or compassionate as the next so choose wisely. Talk to someone who you instinctively feel comfortable with; it might be an aunt or a teacher or a god parent – but ultimately it's far far better to interact with people you know instead of faceless voices in the ether whose objectives may be to your detriment.

...LOOKING FOR LOVE ONLINE

They say you have to kiss a lot of toads before you find your prince, but why would you ever kiss a toad in the first place? I'll tell you why....it's because toads have a way of disguising themselves as princes, and it's only when you get to know them you realise that they are, in

"The person you're flirting with could
be a stark raving lunatic!"

fact, toads. You see, it takes time to get to know someone. I mean, everyone seems great at first don't they! Then....bit by bit....as you become more relaxed around each other you start to see more of their character and all the different sides of their personality. It's only by spending time with a person that you discover if you actually really like them or not. If you realise you don't then no harm done and you move on.

But, how about when you meet someone online? Not a legitimate dating website but Facebook or Tinder I mean? How on earth are you going to form a true opinion of someone based purely on the image you see and the things they say without ever having spent any 'real' time with them? An online stranger can be whoever they want to be, whoever YOU want them to be, and all without having to reveal who they actually are. Let's face it they could be absolutely ANYONE. The person you're flirting with and worse still, falling for, could be a stark raving lunatic! An old man? A sicko! A psycho? It doesn't even bear thinking about.

The Internet is the perfect hiding place for these kinds of predators so for heaven's sake please please please be very careful who you interact with, and be extremely cautious about divulging any personal information....like where you live for instance and OMG never send naked pictures of yourself. In the wrong hands these could become bribery material and you sure as hell don't want that! However, if you think you know better (yes, I was a teenager once!) and believe this person is genuine and plan on physically meeting up with them, you should consider what a dangerous and vulnerable position you could be putting yourself in. You could find yourself in a life-threatening situation or perhaps one that will scar you forever. Of course the obvious advice is to not go at all....or to tell a parent or friend but what use is that?

You: "hey mom, I'm just nipping out to meet a complete stranger I met online!"
Mom: "ok dear, here's hoping he's not a rapist or psychopath. Try not to get killed now!"

Nah. Can't see THAT conversation ever happening. It's pointless because even if you do tell someone what you're doing it doesn't make it any safer; the mystery man is still a mystery man! If you go missing, the only clue the police would have is 'she met some guy online' by which point you'd be in his clutches - too late!!. Perhaps you think 'it'll never happen to me' but y'know what, it's just not worth the risk. There are no shortcuts to finding your soulmate I'm afraid so be aware that the Prince you think you've met online could well turn out to be the King of Toads!

DRUGS AND ALCOHOL

ACTIONS & CONSEQUENCES

I'm not going to lecture you here and nor am I going say those futile words 'just say no' because I'm well aware how pointless that would be. Drugs have become much more accessible and use amongst teenagers is widespread. You guys are drinking more alcohol, to excess, than ever, but while all this may be good fun there are dangers and side-effects you should be aware of. Let me explain a few things about them.

over the pavement and has to be carried home? If so, I think we need to talk! It's not that I don't want you to have a good time, but if you get drunk to the point of almost passing out you won't be able to remember half the evening anyway... so what's the point? If you've spent ages getting ready to go out in the hope of finding yourself a nice boyfriend... only to go out and get completely trashed....none of the decent guys will give you a second look....so what's the point? When was the last time you really fancied someone who was staggeringly drunk....you know, the annoying guy who leans in too far with his booze breath and tries to paw you and slurs gibberish right in your face? Not exactly endearing is it! Now imagine that's you....doing it to a boy....

ALCOHOL

I must admit I do love a glass of wine with dinner. I also like going out with friends and having a few vodka tonic's and occasionally the odd cocktail or two. I enjoy a drink! I don't think there's anything wrong with the odd tipple but you see I don't drink to get drunk....okay, maybe a little merry sometimes, but not drunk. How about you? Are you like me or are you one of those girls who goes out with your friends on a Saturday night, breaks the world record for guzzling as much alcohol as humanly possible, chucks up all

HERE ARE A COUPLE OF TIPS TO MAKE SURE YOU DON'T END UP IN ONE HOT MESS....

♥ EAT before you drink! From my personal experience if I drink on an empty stomach I'll feel the alcohol quickly, and even if I eat half way through the evening it won't sober me up, SO, have a bowl of pasta for instance (carbs are good) before that glass hit's your lips.

♥ Pace yourself. Sip water or have a glass of water between every couple of drinks to give your body time to process the alcohol a bit as you go along. If you don't want to look like a bore have a tonic water or lemonade with ice and a slice which will look like a 'drink' so nobody will know.

♥ It's never a great idea to mix your drinks; you're asking for trouble and almost guaranteeing yourself the hangover from hell. Find what you like and stick to it.

♥ Downing a pint of water before you hit the hay will help massively with that fast-approaching hangover.

♥ Sometimes certain drinks can affect people differently. Some say, for instance 'I can never drink whisky; it makes me really aggressive' or 'I can never drink gin; it makes me feel depressed' so if a particular drink turns you into a monster just avoid it.

♥ If you get that 'oh no I feel quite drunk all of a sudden' feeling then do NOT drink another drop; you don't need to finish the glass. Drink water. One more drink and you risk seeing what you had for dinner all over again. Eeeew!!!

♥ Getting plastered is unsafe. When you're drunk you're vulnerable and you'll make bad decisions. Don't agree to go home or get a lift home with anybody you don't know....anything could happen. Listen to this....

I was chatting to a model one day as I was doing her make-up and she told me about one night when she went to a party. She was about 15 at the time (looked older) and had very little tolerance to alcohol as she rarely drank. Anyway, she got horrendously drunk and ended up on the toilet floor (how mortifying!) while a few other girls tried to help her up. They took her outside where one of her boyfriend's friends offered to drive her around in his car with the window down to help sober her up. They drove off but alarmingly he headed for a secluded country lane and pulled the car up near a deserted farm. He then leaned over to try and kiss her (what an absolute a**ehole) but at that moment she threw up all over him. Hahahah oh brilliant.... but what great timing. He was so horrified he started the car up and drove her back to the party where he dropped her off to her very worried friends....and went home to undoubtedly disinfect his car... and himself.

The point is, what would have happened if she hadn't chucked up? She had put herself in an extremely vulnerable situation; blind drunk with a virtual stranger in the middle of freaking nowhere; I actually can't bear to think about it. Now you know why I say what I say!!!!

HERE ARE A COUPLE OF NASTY THINGS YOU SHOULD KNOW ABOUT ALCOHOL....

Females process alcohol a lot slower than males so you'll get drunk quicker ....so it's pointless trying to keep up with the boys!

Drinking regularly to the point of vomiting will rot your teeth due to the acidity in the alcohol. How d'ya fancy false teeth later in life?

It makes you gain weight. If you think of a large glass of wine as a piece of cake or two glasses as a burger you'll understand where I'm coming from.

It's bad for your skin – alcohol dehydrates the body which is why you look so awful the next day, and it's also why your head feels like it's about to explode.

Overuse of alcohol heightens your risk of all sorts of cancer, especially breast cancer, and can also lead to problems with fertility amongst other hideous things.

"At that moment, she threw up all over him"

Cirrhosis of the liver is a big killer in big drinkers; don't think liver disease won't happen to you – it's a risk you take.

Excessive drinking can lead to alcoholism which can destroy your life. If you start drinking every day or you're worried about your alcohol intake get help quickly while you're still young.

FOR MORE INFORMATION OR HELP REGARDING ALCOHOL CHECK OUT THIS SITE: DRINKAWARE.CO.UK

DRUGS

Recreational drugs alter you mind, and your body, the way you behave, the way you think, the way you feel, and the decisions you make. Different drugs have different effects and strengths, and the affect they have on an individual can vary greatly from one person to the next, depending on your personal tolerance level....and the only way to discover how they'll affect YOU is to try them. This is a very risky business! Your experience could be good or nightmarishly bad, and once in your system there's nothing you can do but to sit and ride it out....like driving a car at high speed minus the steering wheel or brakes. All you can do is wait for it to grind to a halt....eventually. Zikes!

While it's fair to say that drugs can be fun (why else would people do them?) you never get off scott free. The so called 'come-down' is exactly that....it's the opposite of 'fun'. They will leave you feeling tired, moody, empty, irritable, tearful, narky and generally hideous. Worse than that, repeated use of drugs increases the risk of developing schizophrenia (a chronic mental disorder) and drugs like cannabis, cocaine or LSD for instance can trigger panic attacks, depression, paranoia and even psychosis (where you lose contact with reality, hear voices and even contemplate suicide). Doesn't sound that appealing does it!

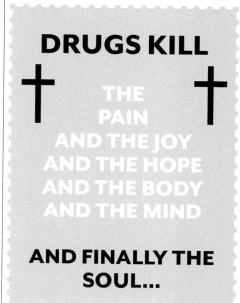

DRUGS KILL

THE PAIN AND THE JOY AND THE HOPE AND THE BODY AND THE MIND

AND FINALLY THE SOUL...

As for the really hard stuff like heroin or crack cocaine; well these are just going to ruin your life. Fact. They're super-duper highly addictive substances and for heaven's sake don't fall into the trap of thinking 'I'll just try it the once' because you'd be conning yourself. To think you can outsmart these kinds of drugs is pure foolishness. Experimenting with drugs is a huge gamble and you should be aware that you're potentially risking your life, or the quality of your life, and possibly your long-term health. For instance, Ketamine (a horse tranquilliser....why anyone would want to put THAT inside their body I'll never know) Growing evidence shows it

lord knows what....sayyyyy....a dash of starch? A spot of caffeine? A sprinkle of....rat poison??? Let's face it, you'll never know what's gone into that pill or that powder or indeed how many filthy kitchen tables or dirty hands have been on it in the making. Eeaughhh!!! So, if you fancy risking putting deadly chemicals in your body....give it a go!

If you have ever seen (or read) 'Bridget Jones -The Edge of Reason' you won't need me to tell you about the dangers, and consequences, of carrying drugs abroad. If this isn't enough to put you off, you should realize that Mark D'Arcy

"She slipped into a coma and after dying twice, survived. Just."

can severely damage the bladder. So, if you fancy the idea of going back into nappies one day....give it a go!

Before making the decision to take any drug it's important to understand the chain of events which occur before they land in your eager paws. It starts at the top with the big boys who probably live in a country you don't even know how to spell, let alone heard of. They handle the purest form of the drug which is sold and exported to wherever, and then it gets passed down a chain of dealers who each cut it or 'lace' it with other substances to pad it out so they each make a profit. By the time it gets to you it could be just 20% pure (or even less)....and 80%

(the one who comes to her aid while she's serving a life sentence in a Thai prison) will not be coming to rescue you. If you get caught, you can kiss your family and friends goodbye and look forward to several years behind bars, and life as you know it is over. No amount of money in the world is worth such a huge risk. Similarly, if anyone ever asks you to carry anything in your suitcase, and I mean anything (you'd be AMAZED at how clever these criminals are at concealing drugs in things) just flatly refuse. If you get a drugs conviction on your record there are many countries which simply won't let you in, ever. So, if you fancy throwing your life away, going to prison or you just never want to travel abroad....give it a go!

On a rather sobering final note, my best friend at school almost died after a night of getting high at a party; her own, to be precise. She'd taken quite a cocktail of drugs and accidentally overdosed. She slipped into a coma and after dying twice and being resuscitated, survived. Just. She incurred permanent brain damage and had to learn to walk and talk again but never to full capacity. She had her whole life ahead of her; a beautiful, clever, vibrant girl whose future had been torn away from her. Please, please, don't let this be you!

LEGAL HIGHS

If it's legal then it must be ok, right? WRONNNNNG!!! Cigarettes are legal and look how many people they kill a year....and they're government regulated! No, you don't want to be messing around with this unpredictable little bunch of rogues. Sadly, it's becoming more and more apparent that they can be just as dangerous, if not more, as illegal drugs, and many lives have been lost as a result of an innocent dabble with one of these 'harmless' substances. My advice? Keep well away.

FOR MORE INFORMATION OR HELP REGARDING DRUGS CHECK OUT THIS SITE: TALKTOFRANK.COM

IF YOU'RE DRINKING OR TAKING DRUGS TO HELP DEAL WITH YOUR PROBLEMS YOU MIGHT WANT TO LOOK AT THIS WEBSITE TOO WHICH LOOKS REALLY HELPFUL: YOUNGMINDS.ORG.UK

CIGARETTES

You may not know this but back in the day smoking was promoted as being 'good for you'!!!. We were led to believe that it not only alleviated stress but it was deemed as elegant and sophisticated... even sexy! Millions of people fell for it and as a result millions have died because of it. If only we had known the serious consequences of smoking back then eh. Happily, we now know better. We know that smoking can kill. I know you know this, but somehow when you're young you never think bad things will happen to you; you feel invincible and that just smoking a few ciggies now and then won't do any harm. The problem is that nicotine is highly addictive, and what starts out as having just the odd one can very easily develop into a full-blown habit which can be extremely difficult to break.

"You'll wonder why you look like your Grandma"

never ever put that first cigarette in your pretty mouth. Smoking is a killer, fact.
IT DOES THIS BY....

💀 Giving you (amongst other things) either cancer of the throat, lips, mouth, tongue, voice box, bladder, kidney, liver, stomach, cervix or pancreas. It's also responsible for 90% of lung cancers.

💀 Putting you at risk of (amongst other things) heart disease, heart attack, stroke, damaged blood vessels,

Fast forward a couple of decades and you're still puffing away....until the day you visit your doctor complaining of chest pains or a persistent cough, or maybe a nasty mouth ulcer that refuses to heal. You go for tests and the results come back....but it's not good news....and in that moment you suddenly wish you had

damaged arteries in the brain, chronic bronchitis, blood clots, bad circulation, osteoporosis (brittle bones), reduced fertility, blocked arteries, pneumonia or emphysema (when the small airways in the lungs are so damaged you need to be hooked up to a bottle of oxygen just to simply breathe)....and death.

If none of this has put you off allow me to appeal to your sense of vanity.

Smoking gives you....

🙂 Terrible ashtray breath.

🙂 Yellow teeth which resemble Cheesy Wotsits!

🙂 Cellulite! The toxins in tobacco will lead to lumpy bumpy orange peel skin.

🙂 Revolting black teeth where the tar builds up on the inside – puuuuuke!

🙂 Brown fingers and orange nails, especially if you roll your own.

🙂 Lines and wrinkles – the chemicals in cigarettes break down the elastin in your skin making your whole body look old and papery.

🙂 A dull complexion – smoking effects your circulation so less oxygen is delivered to the skin making it look grey and lifeless.

🙂 A face like an old boot....well before your time. Smoking ages your skin prematurely by 10 to 20 years. You won't see it for a while yet but it will sneak up on you and when you hit your 40's you'll wonder why you look like your grandma.

🙂 Gum disease resulting in loss of teeth.

🙂 Hollow cheeks and dark circles under your eyes.

If you become addicted to smoking for a long period of time it can affect your circulation so badly that you can end up losing a limb too. If any part of your body has a loss of blood supply the flesh will die, go black, and gangrene will set in. This happened to my lovely Grandmother who had to have half her leg amputated - all because of her daily habit.

HOW TO SAY NO!

I do understand that having read all of this rather frightening (and very real) stuff about smoking that you might still want to try it out; not because you're stupid but because you want to be accepted by your friends and be part of the gang. Smoking, like drinking, underage is about rebellion and discovery which is perfectly normal, but you do have an alternative y'know – you don't have to be LIKE the crowd to be IN the crowd. For instance, the other day my boyfriend's daughter confessed to having the occasional cigarette; she's 16 (I could have cried). Why had she smoked? She wanted to belong (been there, got the T-shirt). Tilly is very popular at school and a lot of girls look up to her; she's in a great position to be a good role model so I suggested something. I said the next time she was offered a cigarette she could just laugh and say 'oh god no – I can't bear cigarettes' and then give a gorgeous non-judgemental smile. If there was still persistence she could then say 'noooo, don't be daft, I don't want to get old and wrinkly before my time thanks' and laugh it off. This way she isn't excluding herself and being mean about those who

"Smoking doesn't make you look cool any more, it makes you look weak"

makes you look weak....and foolish. It's also ridiculously expensive. Let's say a pack of cigarettes is about £9.00 and imagine you eventually smoke twenty a day (average for a proper smoker) seven days a week. Times that by 52 (weeks of the year) equals £3276 a year. What else could you do with that? Go on a designer shopping spree and spoil yourself rotten? Get tickets to the coolest music festivals and have the Best Summer Ever? Buy your first car to cruise around in and go wherever you like? The choices are endless!

do smoke, she's just declaring she's not interested. She will come across as being strong, independent and cool for having the confidence to stand up for her beliefs; she's setting a new bar and hopefully will inspire other friends into following her lead.

On a final note, smoking is SO old fashioned....and certainly NOT sexy! It doesn't make you look cool any more, it

FOR MORE INFORMATION ABOUT SMOKING, THE HEALTH RISKS AND HOW TO STOP, TAKE A LOOK AT THIS WEBSITE BUT WHATEVER YOU DO, PLEASE MAKE SURE YOU DON'T END UP 'DYING FOR A CIGARETTE'. NHS.UK/SMOKEFREE/WHY-QUIT

PANIC ATTACKS

HOW TO COPE AND KISS 'EM GOODBYE!

This term alone almost brings me out in hives! It literally infuriates me that these horrendous and debilitating episodes are called 'PANIC' attacks. Argh.... whoever decided to give them this name has obviously never had one! How do I know? Because I used to get them.... and I can tell you now from first-hand experience they never occurred as a result of 'panicking' about anything; quite the opposite. I'm a strong feisty person but pretty darn laid back, so in my eyes I was the last person to have such a silly, self-indulgent affliction as this – I never

panic about anything! Ptuh!! I mean, I used to think "oh for goodness sake pull yourself together" and wrote people off as being weak. Wow, how wrong was I !!!! The truth is they can happen to anyone, even the strongest person (including you) and are basically the result of prolonged stress. They can start after a bereavement for instance or during tough times like exams, moving house or relationship break ups. Your adrenal system gets so overworked it malfunctions a bit that's all, so before you write somebody off for being a bit pathetic or mad (like I did), just read on and like me, perhaps your view will completely change.

I started having attacks soon after my father passed away; it was very sudden and totally unexpected so it was a massive shock. Of course I was devastated and cried buckets but one day something else happened. I went out for a drive to clear my head and parked up down a quiet country lane for some peace and reflection. I was sitting there when I started to feel a bit dizzy, or fizzy even; kind of light headed and woozy and even a bit tingly. I'd never felt like that before and wondered what on earth was happening to me. Little did I know I was having a 'Panic Attack'. I started to feel a bit scared and things began to escalate until I was sitting there weeping and trembling, my tummy in knots and I felt sick. However, eventually I got my act together and managed to drive home.... not knowing this was the start of many more 'episodes' to come. As time wore on I had more and more attacks which always seemed to occur when I was feeling good, happy even, and often in the middle of having a laugh with friends. Literally, mid giggle, I'd get this very rapid onset of feeling unwell....the stomach churning shaky trembly symptoms I'd always get followed by copious amounts of tears. It was incredibly un-nerving because the attacks would come out of nowhere, made worse by the fact I could never explain them. It was hugely embarrassing and I hated feeling so vulnerable; I thought people would think I was nuts. To be fair, even I thought I was going nuts. It was a hideous time of my life and it was scary....it made me want to stay home to the point I avoided crowded spaces or places I couldn't get away from quickly such as the Underground for instance. ANYWAYYYYY....one day I was in a bookshop with my boyfriend and happened to be standing next to a 'self-help' section while he paid for something. I glanced at the row of books and my eye landed on one which turned out to be my absolute saviour – it quite literally gave me my life back!

I took the book home (all the while my boyfriend sneering at this 'piece of crap' I'd bought) and began to read it while he made us a cup of tea. By the time he walked back in the room I was in tears.... of relief.....because even though I had only read a few pages I discovered that I wasn't losing my mind, I wasn't going nuts after all, but I had actually been suffering from 'Panic Attacks' (although referred to

as Anxiety Attacks; slightly less irritating) Hand on heart, from that day to this I have never had another 'attack'....and that was 20yrs ago!

SO....if you know someone who gets panic attacks or you get them yourself, fear no more!!!! Dr Claire Weekes is at the rescue with her short, inexpensive, simply written but brilliant book 'Self-help For Your Nerves'. She explains why anxiety attacks happen, how they happen, and most importantly how to stop them happening ever again. Many people

"It was hugely embarrassing and I hated feeling so vulnerable"

suffer for years resorting to therapy or anti-depressants but really, once you understand what the hell is going on inside your body, you won't need either!!

If you do have feelings of anxiety or stress you'll find exercise can really help boost your mood too. Take the dog for a long walk, get some fresh air, or run a lovely hot bath with a few drops of calming lavender oil. Even just breathing can help; in through the nose and out through the mouth, slowly, to set your busy mind and heart to rest.

CHAPTER 2

IT'S ALL ABOUT
Your Body

PART 1 –
OUTER YOU

THE SKIN YOU'RE IN – MANAGING SPOTS AND ACNE.

ONE OF THE most upsetting, depressing and confidence-crushing things in a teenage girl's life is bad skin. Whether it's just one giant, pulsating volcanic eruption capable of transmitting messages to Mars, or an overall blot on the landscape of your undeserving face, we believe each one to be ten times the size it actually is. The mere sight of the slightest bump and we're running for the shadows wailing "why me? Why meeeee??" I'll tell you why.....it's your hormones. Dammit!!!! Now while we can't stop them from doing what they do, we can certainly implement a few tactics to help reduce the impact of their roguish ways. So, given that you're not going to take this lying down (face down, into a pillow, crying) I've put together a three-step plan of attack which will no doubt calm things down a bit.

STEP ONE: MY TOP SKINCARE TIPS!

When a zit starts to appear you'll probably do one, or both, of two things. One is to pick it and the other is to cover it in make-up. Picking spots only encourages them to spread which means more make-up….and unless you're meticulous about cleansing your face morning and evening and keeping your make-up brushes or sponges immaculate ….you'll get yourself into a vicious cycle and only make matters worse.

HERE ARE MY TIPS:

The bacteria in spots can be easily spread so if you pick at them and touch your face elsewhere with the same fingers you'll only create more spots. Obviously, it's best not to pick them but we both know you're going to, why kid ourselves, so instead of using your fingers try this. Use a tissue (or a couple of cotton buds) and gently try and ease out any gunk by applying pressure under the spot. If nothing comes out it's not 'ready' so leave it alone or risk making it worse!!! Now soak a cotton wool pad in a naturally antiseptic lotion such as tea tree oil (you can get this from any chemist and it's affordable too) to remove bacteria and soothe the area. If you use a branded product make sure it has anti-bacterial and anti-inflammatory ingredients.

If you have a dark skin tone your skin will be more prone to scarring so pleeease treat it with care. Pick at your peril.

Clean your skin properly. If you rely on face wipes to remove make-up I suggest you try this little experiment: After you've wiped everything off, douse a cotton wool pad with alcohol free toner (rosewater from the chemist would do as it's really gentle and cheap too) sweep it all over your face….then look at the cotton pad. You'll be stunned how much dirt and residue still comes off!!! If you insist on using wipes…finish with a little toner.

Spots can occur due to surface dryness which is why I recommend using an exfoliator. Dead cells sit on

"Obviously it's best not to pick spots, but we both know you're going to"

the skin blocking the pores meaning that any bacteria or excess oil (sebum) can't escape...and before you know it.... boom....another zit! Only exfoliate once or twice a week though as over exfoliating can actually make the problem worse, leading to oversensitive blotchy or itchy skin. Avoid exfoliators containing ground apricot kernels or walnut shells as the rough edges are too harsh.

> "Spots can occur due to surface dryness"

Young skins can be sensitive to overly rich products so if you're prone to breakouts make sure you choose a skincare brand which is simple and light. Overloading your skin with too many serums and creams could be a mistake.

Be careful not to chop and change your skincare products too much as this can lead to what's known as hypersensitivity....and you don't want that!! Your skin will basically go into meltdown and start reacting to anything you put on it. In other words, it will have a tantrum!

Be gentle with your skin. If you wash your face too vigorously, especially in water that's too hot, you risk aggravating and enlarging any inflamed pores.

Beware of products which claim to be 'non-comedogenic' or 'non-acnegenic' (in simple terms this means 'won't clog pores') as these things are very hard to prove in spite of what we're led to believe. If a moisturiser feels heavy, greasy or thick it will most likely 'clog your pores' so opt for one which feels light or thinner to the touch.

Beware of out of date organic creams and potions as the lack of preservatives can make them a prime target for bacteria to grow. If you use these keep your eye on the shelf life date once opened. There's usually an illustration of a lid on the back of the jar which may say 6M or 12M for instance; this indicates how many months from opening before it 'goes off'. In fact, all lotions and potions should have this symbol, organic or not.

Expensive doesn't always mean 'the best'. I've had several high-profile clients (and one very beautiful A-list Hollywood star) tell me their dermatologists have advised ditching the posh creams in favour of much cheaper, dermatological brands found in supermarkets and drugstores. The results, I'm told, can be unbelievably good!

If a product, including make-up, smells like a rose garden or similar, it means it contains scent. This can cause irritation, even if the scent is 'natural'. If you like scent, wear perfume!

♥ Wash your make-up brushes regularly as these are hotbeds for bacteria if not cleaned often enough. Use lukewarm water (hot will melt the glue which holds the hairs in) with a gentle shampoo, specialist brush cleanser or even an anti-bacterial washing up liquid. Wet the brush, dip it in a little cleaner and gently swirl the brush in the palm of your hand with the brush tilted downwards and GENTLY massage the hairs between your thumb and two fingers. Rinse well (I hold the brush under a gently running tap) then squeeze out the water and use something like kitchen roll to soak up the excess. Allow to dry flat (NOT upright in a container with the bristles pointing up... you'll destroy your brushes in time)

♥ If your brushes feel stiff, abrasive or resemble an old birds nest, CLEAN THEM NOW as this indicates a minefield of dirt nestling between those tightly knit hairs! You'll be amazed how soft and lovely they are once cleaned too...and how much more easily your make-up goes on!

"If your brushes resemble an old bird's nest, clean them now!!"

♥ If you use sponges to apply your base you need to be super-dooper meticulous as bacteria will love nothing more than to hunker down in those tiny weeny air pockets. Wash them after every use, boring as it is, if you want to avoid re-infecting your skin every day.

♥ Try and keep your make-up brushes separate from your make-up. Dirty make-up brushes rubbing shoulders with your cosmetics will only spread that invisible spot inducing bacteria.

♥ Your mobile phone is bacteria breeding heaven; it's like catnip to acne! Use a hand sanitiser or carry anti-bacterial wipes in your bag to clean it regularly.

♥ Last, but not least, keep your pillow cases and towels clean! If you're having a breakout you don't want to keep re-infecting your skin do you; it's meant to be 'beauty' sleep after all.

FOR MORE DETAILS ABOUT ACNE AND SKIN PRODUCTS I SUGGEST YOU CHECK OUT PAULA'S CHOICE ONLINE; IT'S A MINE OF INFORMATION ABOUT SKIN CARE AND ONE WHICH I CAN ONLY TOUCH ON IN THIS GUIDE. PAULASCHOICE.COM

STEP TWO:
EAT AND DRINK YOUR
WAY TO BETTER SKIN.

Water. You've heard it a million times; "drink plenty of water; it's good for you" but oh, it's so boring. Water, in my view, is only great when I'm thirsty (when it's the best thing in the world) but at all other times it's just a tasteless, bland liquid which I keep forgetting to drink. Not good ....especially since our bodies are composed of roughly 60% of the stuff. Could this be why every beauty therapist I've ever been to has told me my skin isn't dry it's 'dehydrated'? Considering our skin is the body's largest organ it all starts to make sense. Drinking plenty of water will improve the colour, texture and feel of the skin while it plumps up the cells and helps flush out toxins. If you want to help not just your skin but your entire body too....drink, drink, drink it!!

WHAT ELSE CAN YOU DO? WELL, I'VE DONE A FAIR BIT OF RESEARCH INTO THE CAUSES OF SPOTS AND IT SEEMS THAT THE MAIN FACTORS ARE:

⭐ **Hormones**
⭐ **Stress**
⭐ **Some medicines**
⭐ **Diet**

While it's a common assumption that certain foods can trigger acne you'll be surprised. In fact, greasy foods, which you imagine to be the main culprit, have little or no effect on the skin since the oil in food is different to the oil in the skin (known as sebum). It's more likely the foods listed below which cause problems, but not to the degree you think they do. You could try cutting down on these things and see if it makes any difference to your skin:

⭐ **Sugary foods and drinks**
⭐ **Starchy foods like bread and bagels**
⭐ **Milk and dairy foods (*dairy is notoriously bad for conditions such as eczema for instance!*)**

There is, however, one supplement in particular which I really recommend you take .....and that's Cod Liver Oil. Yes, I know it sounds awful but a) you can take it in capsule form and b) it's pretty tasteless anyway. Cod Liver Oil contains the essential fatty acid Omega3 which your body needs but can't make. It also contains high levels of vitamin D which you mainly get from the sun....but if you don't eat oily fish regularly (such as salmon, tuna, mackerel etc) and you don't spend much time outdoors you could be lacking in these vital body loving elements. The benefits are dazzling as research shows that among its many proven benefits it's FAB for your skin too. I recently urged my friend's 16 year old daughter to take C.L.O. as she was complaining that her hair looked dry and frizzy and her skin was bumpy, spotty and dull. I saw her again a few weeks later and she said she couldn't believe the difference (and nor could I)....she said her nails were longer and stronger as well so she's a complete convert.

If you have acne and it's really bad you can always have a chat with your GP. There are some medications you can take or apply topically which you can't buy over the counter but make sure you're aware of any side effects. I've worked with a fair few models who have resorted to taking a drug called Roaccutane (when all else has failed I might add) which you may have heard of but beware; this is hard core! The list of potential side effects is as long as my arm (or leg...and they're quite long by the way); so much so I'm surprised it's legal.

IF YOU WANT TO KNOW MORE ABOUT THESE HIDEOUS SIDE EFFECTS, TAKE A LOOK AT THE NHS WEBSITE. NHS.CO.UK

"Try cutting down on these things and see if it makes any difference"

STEP THREE: HIDING IT WITH MAKE-UP!

Spots can be really hard to cover up so it helps to know what kind of make-up you should be looking to buy.

First of all, if you just have the odd blemish you might want to simply use a concealer, but if you have more of a widespread breakout you might want to use foundation and a concealer. Either way, they should both match your skin tone exactly. Here are my top tips for disguising those dreaded pimples:

CONCEALER

♥ For spots choose a highly-pigmented concealer with a thick (but not greasy) consistency as they're able to hide any redness. They tend to be drier than more creamy formulations which is perfect as you need something with staying power.

♥ Thinner concealers, such as those which come in a 'pen', are usually intended for use under the eyes where the skin is thinner and more delicate than the rest of the face. Often these contain light reflective particles to help attract and bounce light off the skin to give the illusion of brightness. They can be used to highlight areas of the face too like the cheekbones to give a luminous soft sheen.....so they're the last thing you want anywhere near a spot!! You may as well have an arrow on your face saying 'hey, look at my spot'!

"They're the last thing you want anywhere near a spot"

♥ Look out for 'long wear' formulas which will have superdooper longevity.

♥ Check out 'medicated' concealers which contain zit zapping properties – every little helps!

♥ When shopping for a concealer (or foundation) test the colour on your face, not the back of your hand, as the two will be different shades. When you look in the mirror you shouldn't be able to see where you applied it; if you can it's either too dark or too light.

♥ Apply concealer using a small firm brush for precise application then very gently pat the edges for a seamless finish. You might want to set it with a little translucent powder using another small brush.

♥ Don't use the same concealer you use on your spots under your eyes as it will look too thick and cakey.

♥ If you're using liquid or cream foundation and concealer ALWAYS apply your concealer OVER your foundation. It's pointless doing all that work only to smudge it all over as you apply your base.

♥ If you're using a powder foundation ALWAYS apply your concealer UNDER it.

FOUNDATION

♥ Use the thinnest consistency base you can get away with as I don't believe a very thick mask of make-up looks good at all (and boys hate thick make-up!). Even out your skin with base then apply concealer in the exact same colour over each individual spot.

♥ Set your make-up with a fine, colour free translucent powder using a soft powder puff. Dip the puff in the powder, tap off the excess then roll and press onto the face. Now take a big soft clean fluffy brush to sweep off any excess powder.

♥ If after powdering you think you look 'powdery' try using a facial spritzer to set the make-up and give a smoother finish.

♥ Look for foundations that are transfer resistant (meaning they won't come off on clothes) There are some brilliant products out there so hunt around.

♥ While we all want gorgeous glowing skin it's not realistic if you have a lot of covering up to do...so products like tinted moisturisers and BB creams should be avoided as the textures are too greasy and offer little coverage. Instead, add glow after applying your base and powder using very fine light-reflective highlighters or blushers.

♥ Mineral make-up is a fantastic choice for acne sufferers since it's completely pure, has natural anti-inflammatory properties and covers brilliantly. There are amazing shade ranges available and the textures are very fine.

If you have one zit which is raised (on an otherwise clear skin) you could try turning it into a beauty mark. Take a brown pencil or a touch of light brown eye shadow and gently make a dot in the centre of the spot; it will look like a mole instead.

♡ When you hear that 'mineral make-up is so pure you can sleep in it' I strongly advise you don't....unless of course you want make-up all over your pillow! In fact the quote means it has no talc, filters, chemical dyes or preservatives and can actually benefit the health of your skin.

If you're finding it hard to cope with your acne please don't despair as it will pass. Spots always appear bigger to you than anybody else; nobody is looking at your skin as closely as you....nobody cares as much as you do. To other people you're a girl with a few spots just like thousands of other girls who, like you, will grow out of it.

FIGHTING THE FUZZ

GETTING RID OF UNWANTED HAIR.

As if periods and childbirth weren't enough we also have the ongoing battle with our hair...and I'm not talking the hair on our heads. I'm talking facial hair, leg hair, laaaaaydeee hair (you know where), underarm hair and even....yes even nipple hair! Some have it all but luckily I happen to be very fortunate and have very little unwanted body hair; my skin resembles one of those cats which look like they've been boiled! Still, I do need to do the odd bit of topiary here and there so for me, like all of you, there are options. Let's start with body hair.

SHAVING

It's a total myth that shaving makes the hair grow back more; I've been asked a thousand times but it's simply not true. Hair grows and falls out in cycles; in other words, it doesn't all grow at once then all fall out at once; otherwise we'd be bald most of the time. If you think about it our hair is a mixture of new growth and old growth; the shorter more invisible hairs newer and the longer thicker hairs older. If you were to then shave it all off at once the bulk of it would all start growing back at the same time because most of it would be in some stage of the growth cycle. This is when suddenly you look like you've got more hair and that 'shaving' has made it 'grow back more' when in fact it hasn't; it just seems that way.

So, if you've decided to shave here are a few tips:

Always shave in the opposite direction to hair growth when possible eg. your legs where the hair grows downwards, shave upwards. However underarm hair grows in all different directions so you need to shave in all directions too.

Always wet your skin with warm water to soften the hair and follicle and use a shaving cream or moisturizing soap; you'll need a lather. Shaving dry skin is too abrasive and will not only clog up your razor with dry skin cells you may get razor burn – ouch!

If you run out of shaving products try using olive oil, or if you're already in the bath or shower use hair conditioner. Shampoo is designed to rid hair of dirt and grease so this is too drying; you need something moisturizing.

When your razor becomes blunt, run it along your jeans to sharpen the blades but NOT in the direction you'd use it to shave. Go in the opposite direction about six times and you'll be amazed at the difference.

Always apply a slathering of body moisturizer onto your legs after shaving to avoid dryness. Alternatively use baby oil while your skin is still wet for super silky limbs.

Your razor blades will get clogged with hair as you shave, so every now and then give it a good swish in the water and a flick to keep the razor working efficiently.

Remember shaving is a quick short term solution where the hair is cut off at the surface of the skin. This means the hair will show again quickly and feel stubbly due to the bluntness of the cut.

If you've forgotten to shave say, your underarms, and have no time to jump in the shower I have a brilliant tip. Simply use talcum powder (which has a silky feel) on dry skin and the razor will glide along leaving you super smooth and cut free without the use of any water or foam.

WAXING

ONE TWO THREE AAAGH!!

If you want longer term results than shaving offers you might want to think about waxing....if you have a high pain threshold, that is! Waxing involves spreading a thin layer of hot wax onto the skin with a wooden spatula, pressing a strip of fabric over it, then ripping it off in the opposite direction the hair grows in. Sounds painful? It is. Well, it is but it's quick and I believe you get used to it over time. I've had waxing in a salon and I've tried it at home but really you can get into all worlds of trouble doing it yourself, so if you're not super dexterous and organized, have it done professionally. One major downside worth mentioning (other than the paaaaain) is that you need to wait until the hair re-grows to a certain length before waxing again.... and typically you're bound to get a hot date the day before you go, and run the risk of exposing your barbed wire legs!!! On the up-side though the results last much longer than shaving. Instead of the hair being cut off at the surface (making it blunt and stubbly), the hair is pulled out from the root so it takes longer to reappear (between two to six weeks) and when it does, the brand new hair has a really fine tip making it way softer. This is great for holidays when you're in a bikini every day and don't want to have to shave....especially if you're sunburned. I also think waxing is quite a good solution if you're particularly hairy, as shaving every single day would be a real chore.

Over time with continual waxing the hair grows back less; I think the follicle realises it's simply fighting a losing battle, yassss!! If you DO give waxing a go it's highly recommended to avoid going in the sun, using a scrub or having a hot bath for 24hrs afterwards.

Both shaving and waxing can lead to ingrown hairs which can be sore and always look awful. This is when the hair either can't break through the surface of the skin or it simply grows back inwards. Ways to avoid this are by exfoliating with a body scrub regularly to remove dead skin cells, or by using a product such as Tend Skin a couple of times a day which is widely recommended to treat them. Also avoid having a wax the week before your period; you're more sensitive then so it'll hurt more - why torture yourself!

COLD WAX STRIPS

These are pre-waxed strips of paper which you warm between your hands for a minute or two. You then peel the backing off, press onto the skin and rip off in the opposite direction to hair growth. Do they work? Hmm, kinda sorta. I can't imagine these working so well on strong hair and you need to use quite a few and go over the same spot a couple of times. Not bad for a quick fix but generally.....meh!

EPILATORS

I tried using one of these feisty contraptions when they first came out and my eyes still water at the memory. These electronic devices basically yank out the hairs en masse as you glide the machine over your skin; imagine between 20 and 40 miniature tweezers plucking away at incredible speed and you've got it. Like waxing, the hair comes out from the root so the results last the same amount of time, however, I personally find them more painful. On the plus side, they can grab hairs only a millimetre long which (better than waxing) is rather impressive. They're an investment and think of the money you'll save on waxing.

DELAPITORY CREAM

To be honest I've never had much success with these and I hardly have any excess hair! Basically, these creams contain a chemical which dissolves the hair shaft in a few minutes (supposedly). You apply them then sit around and wait (looking rather silly I might add – make sure you lock the bathroom door) during which time you'll wish you had a clothes peg to hand to block your nose from the rather noxious stink of melting hair; eeeeewww!!! Once the said time has elapsed you then scrape the cream off with the spatula thingy to reveal (supposedly) smooth hair free limbs. Once you've tidied up the excess hairs that didn't dissolve and removed the peg from your nose you'll want to apply moisturizer....but you can't.....for about 24hrs. Now, as far as hair removal goes I ask you, does this sound like a good option? Nah.

LASERS

If you've got money to spend then this, in my opinion, is the way forward. It's expensive as you'll need a course of treatments but you'll get great results. Simply put, lasers kill the hair and eventually they don't grow back any more – yippeeee!! However, you'll need a few treatments (around 6 to 8) and I have to say in time some hairs do grow back BUT, I find just the odd top up a couple of times a year will keep you silky as an otters pocket. If you suffer from ingrown hairs you can say goodbye to those too which is great especially for your bikini line and underarm. Does it hurt? It's like someone pinging an elastic band on you; milliseconds of pain but certainly bearable. Seeing as this cost a few £££'s why not ask for a course of treatments for your 18th birthday? Better than your folks shelling out a lump sum in one go and better than you saving up for ages eh. Just a thought.

"You run the risk of exposing your barbed wire legs!"

FACIAL HAIR

Do you look like a Wookie or do you have skin like a freshly picked peach? Either way everyone has facial hair and it's completely normal. In fact, the only parts of the skin which are hair free are the palms of the hands and the soles of the feet!

Years ago, while on a photo shoot, I couldn't help but notice something kinda odd about the fashion stylist. She was very pretty but she had this odd kind of alien look to her – I couldn't for the life of me work out what it was that jarred so much and I just kept staring at her, poor girl; couldn't help it (she must have thought I was some sort of lunatic....or fancied her). Anyway, as the day wore on we chatted about makeup and beauty and she told me that she regularly had all of her facial hair waxed off – the whole face! She was American and told me it was commonplace in the States and that tonnes of girls did it, even if they weren't visibly hairy. As soon as she said it, it seemed so obvious....but it looked odd. Her skin had a waxy shiny feel to it and I have to say.....it didn't look....natural. You see what you don't realize is that for skin to look like skin it has to have even the most invisible veil of hair on it, and I'll tell you now, trying to get makeup to stick onto a bald skin is a nightmare. It's like applying foundation onto glass – it slips – pain in the butt! SO, before you go attacking your face with hair removal treatments I advise you to only target the problem areas and leave the rest alone.

Problem areas for facial hair are usually the upper lip, chin, eyebrows and sides of the face from ear to jawline. I'd say only remove it IF it's particularly visible or long or if it's affecting your confidence, but certainly don't remove it just because your friends do it or indeed because you think 'that's what all girls do' – they don't!

So, if your hair is more 'forest' than 'fuzz' here are your options:

⭐ Waxing – this works in the same way that waxing body hair works except using smaller amounts of wax and smaller strips of fabric. The same pros and cons but I think the main one being the bit where you have to wait until the hairs are long enough before waxing again....although they do grow back finer. Waxing isn't usually recommended for darker skin tones as it can cause discolouration so, if that's you, opt for another method.

⭐ Depilatory Cream – a really quick, cheap and easy method to do yourself in the privacy of your home. In my experience this works better on fine facial hair than it does on more stubborn body hair. Hair grows back a tad stubbly and you may need to do it every couple of weeks but I'd certainly give it a go if you're low on budget and want to keep it to yourself.

⭐ Tweezers – really you'd only use tweezers for eyebrows or the odd hair on your chin maybe. To use tweezers over a larger area of longer hair would be difficult and most time consuming. Tweezing hair pulls the hair from the root so it takes longer for the hair to grow back.

⭐ Threading – yikes I've never tried this but soooo many girls I know have it done so it can't be all that painful. Threading involves a length of cotton and a skilled beautician who plucks the hair from your face as the cotton is twizzled back and forth over the skin. Dozens of hairs are pulled out at a time but unlike plucking with tweezers it leaves zero behind...even the wispy downy hairs are removed. Great for the upper lip and eyebrows providing the beautician knows what she's doing.

⭐ Lasers – check out the section above about body hair removal as it's the same thing. Again, this is a costly method but if you really do have excessive hair and it's really getting you down then it's an investment in yourself; after all people see your face the whole time whereas your legs for instance are often covered up beneath jeans or trousers. You need about 4 weeks between treatments and you'll have to shave in between; you can't pluck or wax so bear this in mind.

⭐ IPL – this stands for Intense Pulsed Light and works in a similar way to Lasers (using various light wavelengths instead of one) I hear it's probably better for darker skin and fairer hair and is less painful. You need a considerably longer gap between treatments than Lasers but it does also offer reduced, if not permanent, elimination of hair regrowth.

⭐ Electrolysis – a time consuming, costly but most effective way to destroy the enemy!! A fine needle is inserted into each hair follicle (well I did say 'time consuming') where a tiny jolt of electricity shoots down and kills the hair – zap! You'll

"Many mini shocks later, you'll be permanently hair free"

need several sessions but eventually, many mini shocks later, you'll be permanently hair free – yippeeeeeeeee!!

⭐ Bleaching - for those who aren't bothered about the presence of hair itself and more concerned about the colour of it you can always bleach it....at home... yourself...quick, cheap and easy! I've used 'Jolen' crème bleach in my makeup kit for years for those occasional requests for 'barely-there brows'. It's been around for over 50yrs and can be used on both facial hair and body hair and you can buy it just about anywhere.

If any of you are wondering why I'm not suggesting shaving as an option it's because it's just a really bad idea...unless you want man stubble and a six o'clock shadow! Just.....don't!!

#TIP

Haven't got a brow brush? Take an old mascara wand and thoroughly wash it in warm water and washing up liquid to remove any remaining mascara. You'll now have a fresh clean spiral brush to tidy your brows and your lashes...for free!

EYEBROWS

FINALLY – A WORD ON EYEBROWS!!! OH PLEASE READ THIS!!!!

If there's one thing that will affect the way you look it's your eyebrows.....too bushy they will overwhelm your face.... but over-plucked, tweezed or threaded and you'll look.....ummm....weird! The problem with shaping brows is that you can very easily get out of control, and after time completely lose the natural basic shape....which in turn can lead to all sorts of browmares (like nightmares but with brows, instead of....erm....nights) Anyhow, if you stick to my guide you won't go far wrong.

If you look at this image (**see opposite**) it indicates where your brows should start and finish and ideally where the top of the arc should be. Use a slim brush or pencil and place it along the side of the nostril and the inner corner of the eye (**A**). When these two points are aligned follow up along the guideline and it will show where your brows should begin. Remove any hairs beyond this point. Apply the same rule as per the diagram to find the ideal end-point to your brows (**C**). Map out where the arch looks best as the line (**B**) passes the pupil of your eye (this should be enhanced with make-up!)

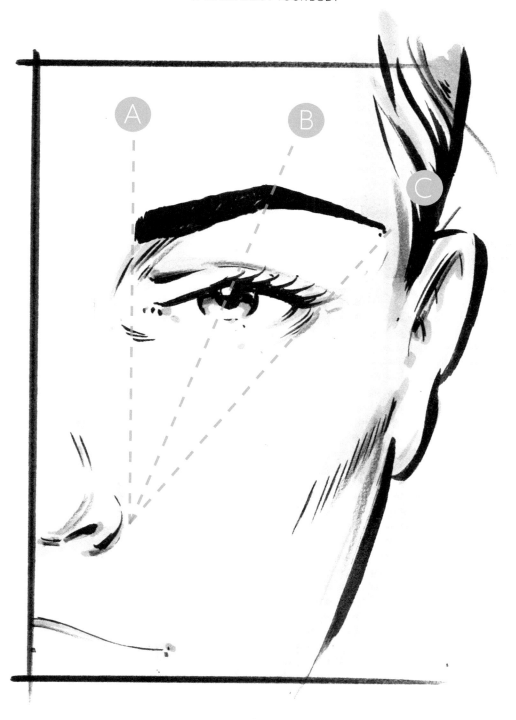

Never pluck your brows....

♥ Too far back at the centre....the further they are apart the more vacant you will look.

♥ Too thinly – the thinner they are the harder you will look.

♥ Too short at the ends – the shorter they become the more stunned you will look.

♥ So they resemble tadpoles or hockey sticks – they should taper from thicker where they begin to finer at the ends in one heavenly arc of loveliness.

♥ From the top – a soft top line looks nice and works well with a nice sharp clean line underneath.

♥ In the opposite direction that they grow – you'll damage the follicle and the hair will regrow in a different direction. Always pluck in the direction they grow.

♥ Without checking the shape after every two or three hairs. Even one or two hairs can make a world of difference and it's easy to get out of control here. Use a brow brush or comb to push hairs in place as you go along before continuing your mission.

♥ One of the dangers of shaping your brows is that over time, bit by bit, hair by hair, if you're not careful your brows can become shorter and shorter and thinner and thinner. Keep your eye on this by only ever removing the regrowth with a pair of good tweezers. However, if you prefer a salon wax or threading, make sure your beautician is vigilant about doing the same by asking her to ONLY remove the new hairs. If not, even the tiniest extra bit on each visit can eventually result in comical little cartoon arcs instead of the beautifully sculpted brows you began with! I've seen this happen to a few of my friends who are now desperately trying to grow them back.

If you're Afro-Caribbean your brow hairs will most probably be curly and hard to tweeze. Not only that but you risk scarring your skin so the best way to create a beautiful brow is to use a cheap, disposable, brow razor. They look like this and can be found at most hair supply stores if not in your local chemist:

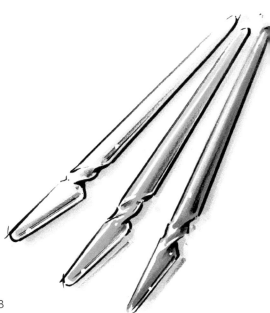

A great tip for creating a perfect brow shape is to use a white eye pencil to cover the hairs you'd like to take off, blocking them out until you form the shape you desire. Now either tweeze the hair, or, if using a brow razor, place it flat against your skin, and with your free hand secure the brow area firmly. Gently nudge the razor against the direction of growth (as you would when shaving legs) and remove all the hairs covered by the white pencil. Use a little toner to remove any remaining pencil, and you should be left with the exact shape brows you want....all this and pain free too!

FOR TIPS ON HOW TO PERFECT YOUR NEWLY SHAPED BROWS WITH MAKE-UP, HEAD OVER TO THE MAKE-UP SECTION IN CHAPTER 3 'IT'S ALL ABOUT FACE'.

PUBIC HAIR

In the 70's I don't think anybody, male or female, gave a second thought to the state of their....umm....intimate hair? Pfft – have no idea what to call it really do you? Either way it sounds silly, medical or downright pornographic! Call it what you will, back in the day it was left to grow wild and free and nobody cared a toss. However, as the decades have passed, the fashion for your 'personal' hairstyle has changed....it's become less and less, bit by bit, until now it's deemed simply polite to have nothing there at all.....or maybe just a precarious little strip.....like a lonesome exclamation mark suspended there beneath your navel without it's dot! Dear me – the pressure we are under to get it right eh....and where do you go from 'nothing' I ask? Surely 'back to something', no? I can only hope.

"A full on 'Brazilian' will only make your hips look wider...if that's an issue"

Like all things, styles change, and like fashion, not everybody likes the same look, so my advice to you is to not be swayed by what you THINK you should have, and go with what you think looks nice. Removing pubic hair is painful....

especially when you have it all ripped off by some masochistic waxing maniac who you've never met before and whose only goal is to see her own reflection in your shiny bald patch down below. Ooh no, not for me! Aside from that, there's the itchy scratchy regrowth and the ingrown hairs.....not pretty, not nice. All I'm saying is don't take your lead from page 3 girls or porn stars, and take into account the rather high maintenance of an overly coiffed hair-do. A full on 'Brazilian' will also make your hips look wider...if that's an issue.....as there's nothing to 'draw the eye in' so to speak. Anyway, I really don't see what's wrong with a tidy, closely shorn feminine lawn in a neat little triangle and besides, before you know it that will be 'back in fashion'.

'OTHER' HAIR

Body hair has a nasty habit of popping up precisely where you want it the least..... we're talking chest hair and nipple hair! It's quite common for a girl to have the odd bit of nipple hair and even a few hairs on the chest in between the breasts – it's more common than you think. Simply pluck these out with tweezers or you could try electrolysis or even laser treatments. However, I wouldn't advise waxing as the nipples can be quite sensitive and nooooo-body wants hot wax there do they.

BODYLICIOUS

THE KEY TO BEAUTIFUL LIMBS

SMOOTH OPERATOR!

Nothing feels nicer than soft supple silky skin, and now that you've de-fuzzed yourself there are still a few things you can do for extra smoothness. Things like air conditioning and central heating can dry out and dehydrate our skins so here's how to combat that:

Use a moisturizing body wash instead of regular soap.

Use a loofah or a bath brush in the bath or shower to help stimulate the skin and exfoliate it.

Try using a body scrub to help remove dead skin cells which make the skin feel dry and rough.

As soon as you step out the bath or shower apply body oil (Baby Oil works well if you can't afford something more luxurious) onto wet skin; it's much easier to apply this way and leaves you gorgeously soft without feeling oily.

Always apply body moisturizer after bathing and give it a good rub in to stimulate the circulation.

If you run out of moisturizer add a few drops of oil into your bath water instead (providing you're not planning on rinsing your hair in it).

Choose a nice rich body moisturizer especially on your shins, knees and elbows which tend to be drier. Some of the dermatological drugstore brands do great affordable ranges and perform better than those super cheap overly scented ones!

When you're going out apply a few drops of Dry Body Oil onto your arms and legs; it won't leave an oily residue but still make your skin glow.

If you have red pimply rough upper arms....or thighs....you probably have something called Keratosis Polaris.... or what's more commonly known as 'Chicken Skin'. Charming! It usually occurs in puberty and disappears in adulthood (massive PHEW!) and it signifies a lack of essential Omega 3 fatty acids in your diet and/or poor circulation. It's simply a build-up of Keratin which blocks the tiny hair follicles in your skin producing red bumps. Help fix this by eating oily fish such as tuna, salmon and mackerel a couple of times a week and try flaxseeds and walnuts to snack on too. Other great sources of Omega 3's are veggies like sprouts and cauliflower or alternatively taking a daily supplement of Cod Liver Oil works wonders. Using a body scrub, loofah or exfoliating glove regularly will also help smooth your limbs followed with a rich body cream slathered on afterwards. Follow these steps and you'll really see a difference!

BEAUTIFULLY BRONZED

I have a typical British white girl skin tone. In the summer, I go a lovely golden brown shade, but come the winter it's not quite so pretty when my skin resembles a bowl of cold grey porridge (unlike some girls whose pale creamy porcelain skin is simply beautiful). If you're like me though and you look only half alive without a bit of colour, all is not lost!!! Thank god for fake tan!!!!

Fake tan is the safest and best route to achieving a natural looking bronzed bod, and there are loads of great products out there to help us do this. There's a huge choice in fact which can be a bit daunting but they mainly fall into a few small categories:

⭐Tinted self-tan body lotions – these are body creams with a hint of fake tan which you can apply every day as you would a normal moisturiser. They're great especially in the winter time when you just want a subtle hint of colour to make you look healthier. Make sure you wash your hands after each application or risk strange looking brown palms.

⭐Instant wash off formulas – these provide immediate colour and are great for those last-minute occasions when you need instantly brown limbs. You need to apply these quickly and evenly as they dry pretty fast. Just be careful not to get your skin wet if they're not waterproof; I've actually seen girls with streaky legs after they've been caught out in a rain storm!

⭐Gradual Tanners – these can be creams, lotions, gels or sprays which you apply evenly using gloves or a mitt then wait a few hours for the colour to develop. Some are colourless, but I prefer the tinted ones as it's easier to see where you've applied them, plus you get a slight tinge of colour straight away.

⭐Gradual wash off formulas – these are pretty fool-proof as you can slap them on all over and not worry too much about streaking, providing every bit of skin has some coverage. You wait a few hours (they tend to be dark in colour so you'll look pretty freaky) then shower the product off.....revealing a beautifully even colour underneath with no streaks. Be warned though; I've known girls to apply products like this but leave the house without the 'washing off' bit; they look like they've been dipped in gravy!

☆Fair skin tanners – some brands cater specifically for very fair skins which can easily look orangey with regular tanning products. No more tangerine stripes!

☆Self-tan wipes – these are impregnated with fake tan which you swipe over your skin for instant results. Great for travel or festivals as they're lightweight, disposable and won't leak.

HOW TO APPLY – STEP BY STEP.

Here's my step by step guide how to apply fake tan evenly without looking like you've been rugby tackled in the mud by an octopus:

♥ Be prepared! Tie your hair up and out of the way and have everything you need to hand. Remove all jewellery and have a loose garment or old T shirt nearby to pop on afterwards until the fake tan dries.

♥ Take a bath or shower and exfoliate your body first paying extra attention to any dry patches such as knees and elbows. These are places where FT (fake tan) will accumulate and where it looks like the octopus has won!

♥ Next apply a light body moisturizer; something that will sink in but leave you with a nice even surface all over. You may have to wait ten minutes for it to absorb properly.

♥ If you haven't got a tanning mitt take a pair of disposable latex gloves or regular washing up gloves and put them on. Using gloves distributes the FT much more easily and evenly, and eliminates the risk of the palms of your hands looking bright orange for days afterwards.

If, somehow, you've managed to still get an unwanted brown streak anywhere, try using a pumice stone to remove it. Use a very gentle swirly motion to lightly buff off those pesky patches – do it in the bath when your skin is wet.

♥ Starting with the lower part of the legs massage a good splodge of FT all over the fronts and backs in circular motions. Do this quite vigorously to get it even.

♥ Add a little bit to your feet; still buffing in circular motions but make sure you don't get a build up between your toes or around the nail cuticle. If so you're using got too much product so quickly wipe it off with a tissue where there's any excess. Blend the FT out to the sides and make sure you blend it down the back of the heel.

💜 Now repeat this continuing with your thighs then bottom, tummy....and work your way up to the neck and under the jaw line continuing to use firm circular movements.

💜 Next do your arms down to the wrists.

💜 If you're tanning your body your face should match, so providing the FT can be used on the face apply a smaller amount all over it. Use small circular motions but try not to get it clogged into your brow hair as you'll end up with an orange halo around your eyebrows. Same goes for the hairline; just blend the FT out towards the hairline without going into the hair....all this takes a bit of practice and trial and error!

💜 Finally, remove the gloves and apply a blob of FT onto the back of one hand. Now use the backs of both hands against each other to blend the FT evenly over the hands and fingers, again making sure you don't get a build up between the joints or nail beds. Rub the insides of the wrists together to make sure it's all blended there nicely too.

💜 Pop your loose-fitting clothes on (ones you don't care about) and try not to get any part of your skin wet for an hour or more or as per the instructions.

💜 Later in the day, stand back and admire your flawless handiwork and muse over the fact you've saved yourself a fortune at a tanning salon!!

#TIP

💜 Don't forget about your ears! Distribute a tiny bit of product between your fingers and massage over your ears or else they'll stand out like bright white handles on the side of your head!

If it's your palms which have gone bright orange (because you didn't take my advice about the gloves – lol) then celebrity tanmeister James Read suggests rubbing them together with either shaving foam or toothpaste (yes, really) for about ten minutes until the pigment dissolves. Love it!

If none of this 'fake tan' malarkey appeals to you and you're hell bent on a session of sun bed treatments, you should really check out the cancer research website before you do. Using sun beds before the age of 35 increases your risk of developing melanoma skin cancer by 60% which I think is very frightening. Why risk losing your life or a limb for the sake of being a shade or two darker when there are so many great alternatives on offer.

IF YOU'RE NOT CONVINCED, READ WHAT THESE PEOPLE HAVE TO SAY. SUNSMART.ORG.UK

PERSONAL HYGIENE

HOW NOT TO SMELL LIKE A WILDEBEEST!

The problem with B.O. and bad breath is that nobody ever tells you you've got it! Your friends will endure it and loathe it but find it almost impossible to tell you for fear of hurting your feelings.....and boys.... well they'll take one sniff and head for the nearest exit. The only way you can counteract this potential hazardous zone is to head it off at the pass, before it happens, and pay attention to your personal cleanliness. Unless you want to clear a room in five seconds flat, read on…

PONGY PITS?

For starters, fresh sweat doesn't smell. However, if you sweat and don't bathe, the bacteria which lives naturally on your skin will dine out on the sweat and it's this that makes you pong. By the same token, if you do bathe but then, the next day put the same item of clothing on you sweated in the day before, your body heat will warm up the dried sweat, reignite the bacteria and boom, Miss Pongy reigns again! The simple solution is to bathe daily but to also use a deodorant, or better still an 'antiperspirant deodorant' which helps minimize the actual sweating while also killing off the unpleasant odour (hence 'de-odor-ant') So, when you're in the chemist look for one which does both; simples! If you suffer from excess sweating (poor you) there are much stronger products available like Perspirex or Driclor which help combat those embarrassing damp patches.

Buy an antiperspirant deodorant with the most neutral scent. Any added perfume will smell cheap and chemical!

I'm well aware that there are a whole host of deodorants especially made for vaginas too – HA! You hear me laugh! I couldn't think of anything worse than to spritz your rather sensitive special place with some nasty pungent spray so that you smell like you've accidentally sat on a bowl of granny's pot pourri. This area isn't like your armpit – it's a whole different world and anything highly scented down there can trigger thrush and god knows what. In fact, so can highly scented soaps so my advice to you is to avoid at all costs. If you wash regularly you won't need any of these awful chemicals to make you smell good....in that department you should smell natural; not of a mountain primrose or a winter lily....nooooo.....it's just plain wrong. I ask you, would you wear the cheapest smelling perfume you could find on your neck on a hot date? No. So why douse yourself in it everywhere else? Same goes for Body Spray; wear nice perfume instead!

#TIP

When buying clothes be aware of what they're made of. Manmade fibres don't allow your skin to breathe as much as natural fibres like cotton, wool or silk. Synthetic fabrics, especially worn close to the sweatier areas like the armpit or feet, will soon get a bit whiffy and may be more difficult to erase smells from. Don't say I didn't warn ya!

BREATH OF DEATH?

Moving on to bad breath - I almost think this is worse than B.O. so let's make sure you don't get it.

✓ Clean your teeth at least twice a day and have regular dental check-ups. Bad teeth and plaque (which causes gum disease) are a breeding ground for bacteria which emit that awful stinky gas.

✓ Watch what you eat especially before a hot date or job interview – garlic is delicious but boy can it make your breath whiff. Apparently raw garlic is more pungent than cooked...so maybe say no to the hummus girls or avoid altogether!

✓ Smoking – the funny thing is that smokers have no idea how much of a stench they emit after having even one cigarette. The times I've done a model's make-up just after she's popped out for a Marlboro Light and almost swooned at the smell afterwards is incalculable.

Even if they chew gum (which I insist upon now) or clean their teeth the underlying 'air du fag' remains for quite a while.... and poor old me has my face right next to theirs too eeeeuuuuughhhhh!!!!! I honestly could never date a smoker – it just turns my stomach. The answer to ashtray breath is 'don't smoke'.

✓ Diets – low carb diets cause the body to break down fat which in turn produces a chemical which smells, so in this case bad breath comes from the stomach. Damn – you can't win eh! However, some vegetables such as celery, carrots and apples are said to counteract it as are many herbs such as parsley (which you can chew) or mint leaves (steep in hot water to make mint tea).

✓ Illnesses - certain types of illnesses and medications can give you bad breath but what can you do; you need to take your medicine right? How about carrying a pocket size breath freshener or a pack of strong mints? I'd suggest chewing gum too, but not only can it cause bloating (due to the amount of excess air you swallow while chewing), but it also tricks your stomach into thinking food is coming....which triggers an overproduction of digestive acid. No girl wants to be bloated AND smelly do they!

✓ Sugar – sugary food and sugary drinks like Coke etc cause plaque which rots your teeth, causes gum disease and....bad breath. Cut down or at least clean your gnashers after having this evil (but irritatingly yummy) substance.

HAIR OF THE DOG?

Now we've mastered the art of smelling like a lovely girl and not a farm animal, let's turn our thoughts to our hair. Greasy hair not only looks revolting but also smells a bit like the bottom of a hamsters cage....or is that just me? You know what I mean; it smells a bit fusty and earthy and if you've been in a smoky room or a smelly restaurant the night before.... it'll smell of that too. Imagine; grease + curry + nicotine + sweat = mm-ummmmhhh, special!! There have been countless times when the hair stylist on a shoot has had to curl or straighten a model's dirty hair; as soon as the heat hits the grease the smell it emits is gag-making. Always make the effort to give your hair a wash, especially if you're planning on getting up close and personal with someone!! Here are my top 10 hair washing tips:

Choose a shampoo which suits your hair type as some will be more astringent or heavier than others. For instance, using a rich shampoo for thick coarse hair on fine hair will be too heavy making the hair go flat and greasy more quickly. Similarly, a shampoo for fine hair on thick coarse hair won't be cleansing or nourishing enough resulting in dull looking hair.

Don't over scrub your scalp or wash your hair too vigorously as this will only stimulate the sebaceous glands and make them produce more oil (as will water which is too hot)

Only apply conditioner from the mid lengths down. The roots are automatically moisturized by the natural oils which kick into action soon after washing.

Hair is more elastic when it's wet and more fragile so don't go yanking your brush through it or you'll get breakage. Use a wide tooth comb or special de-tangling brush instead.

Always comb any tangles out from below the knot, not above it. If you try and tease the knot out from the top pulling it down the length of the hair you'll find it harder to remove while causing damage too. Teasing out from underneath the knot is much quicker and more gentle. Use this technique on wet or dry hair.

#TIP

Got chewing gum in your hair? Massage in some vegetable oil and watch it disintegrate away with ease!

It's a MYTH hair products repair split ends; they just smooth them down so you think they're repaired. Once an end is split it's game over...it's the end of the end (lol), and the only way to get rid is to have a trim every 6-8 weeks. If left unattended the split will only move further up the hair shaft and make matters worse.

♥ Shampoo is designed to rid hair of grease, and conditioner is designed to give it moisture. Therefore, if you're on a budget, it's always worth spending more money on a shampoo than a conditioner as a conditioner will never damage your hair...whereas a shampoo might just strip it or dry it out.

♥ If you wash your hair in the bath make sure you do the final rinse in fresh clean water. It's pointless rinsing it in the water which has shampoo, soap, and bits of hair from shaving your legs in it! Maybe take a plastic jug in there if you only have a static shower head.

♥ Instead of towel drying your hair by rubbing it like crazy try using the towel to squeeze the excess water out instead. This is far less abrasive to the hair, especially if it's curly.

♥ Wait until wet hair is about 70% dry before trying to style it. Use your dryer and your fingers to rough dry it to reduce the bulk of the moisture first. This makes styling quicker and reduces the risk of damaging or parching your lovely locks by scorching the hair with too much direct heat.

While dry shampoo is a great way to quickly deal with dirty hair in zero time, it's also a brilliant way to add volume to clean flat or fine hair too (a trick session stylists have used for years) Give your hair a good shake through with your fingers after applying to make sure there are no dusty looking patches!

When it comes to styling your hair there's a vast array of products on offer to turn your hair into a thing of real beauty. With a bit of time, effort, trial and error you can have the glorious mane you've always longed for. Just be careful of those heated appliances though! Use a heat protecting spray and don't leave tongs or straighteners in place for too long; keep them moving to reduce the risk of damaging the hair.....oh....and please unplug them afterwards!!!!

For some of you, your hair will always be your nemesis! Unruly locks of frizzy or stubbornly curly hair can drive even the sweetest teen (or grown woman, come to that) to the edge of reason. Oh, how I wish I'd invented the so called 'Brazilian Blow Dry'; I'd be totally minted by now! This is a rather pricy hair treatment which must be done in a salon, takes about an hour and lasts up to about three months. It smooths and tames all types

> ".. Gorgeous hair is the best Revenge !" ..

of stubborn waves and leaves you with gorgeous swishy swathes of shiny hair although, some say it's not all good news. Some report hair loss and/or brittleness so be warned. Do your research and don't have it done more than three times a year. Like with most salon beauty treatments, there's always an element of risk.

A HAIRY SCARY WARNING!!

While on the subject of risk, there's something else you really need to know. If you plan on colouring your hair at home you'll see on the box it advises you to do what's called a 'patch test'. A patch test is where a small amount of product is placed on a discreet area of skin such as behind your ear or the back of the neck and then left for 24 hours to see if there's

any kind of allergic reaction. While this sounds boring I strongly suggest you take heed and follow their advice. Sometimes, the chemicals in the dye can result in anything from a rash, to itchy skin, to a

face which blows up like a balloon and you end up looking like a sunburnt sumo wrestler with a hangover. If you don't believe me search Google images for 'hair dye allergies' and if that doesn't make you sit up and take note I don't know what will. Those pictures are shocking! In fact, most good hair salons insist on a patch test before agreeing to colour anybody's hair as the risk is too catastrophic, so if you tend to have sensitive skin or are prone to allergies you should insist on one. Like with many beauty products these occurrences are rare, but it's always wise to play it safe – you just never know!

LIGHTING UP THE ROOM....

WITH YOUR SMILE

Have you ever noticed how many people have yellowy manky teeth? Years ago, I invested in a teeth whitening kit; the one where the dentist makes plastic trays which you then fill with bleach, shove on your teeth and sleep in overnight for about ten days. During this process, I really started looking at other people's gnashers, I couldn't help it, and was amazed at what I saw. It seemed that half the population didn't own a toothbrush!! Ok I might be exaggerating but really, there was a lot of amber fang going on and oh my lord the plaque...the visible plaque. Pukerama!!!!

You maybe don't realize how much people look at your mouth when you talk to them; they focus on your eyes and lips to help interpret the context of what you're saying as well as the actual words.....so if you think about it....it's pretty important you look after your teeth. Lovely sparkly white teeth look really attractive, even if they're not perfectly formed – they brighten up your face and make you infinitely more kissable! I recommend a twice yearly visit to the

dental hygienist to get rid of any plaque (which causes tooth decay, gum disease, loss of teeth, and bad breath) and if you smoke, any black tar residue. Brush twice a day with a good toothbrush (a sonic electric toothbrush at best) renewing the heads every three months and use a protective fluoride toothpaste. If you happen to have a fear of the dentist you might want to consider the alternative.... of no teeth....or false teeth...in a glass... beside your bed at night. Just think, you could say goodnight to your own teeth!!

IMPLANTS & FILLERS

WHY BIGGER ISN'T ALWAYS BETTER

BREAST IMPLANTS

I was a late developer; I didn't start my periods until I was 14 years old and it seemed to take a lifetime for my boobs to make an appearance. SO frustrating – I thought it'd never happen! When it did I was pretty happy with my figure and presumed it'd stay that way for years. However, your body changes a fair bit over time and my once 32C's are now rather voluptuous 34DD's....and depending on the make of bra I once even bought an E cup!!!! Zikes!!!! Who knew! But that's just the point – you don't know how your body's going to change. To be honest I wish they were a bit smaller; I think clothes hang better....big boobs limit what you can wear and often a little top which looks cool on someone else will just look plain tarty on me. Having said

that I know that many of you might want big boobs and are perhaps playing with the idea of having implants one day.

Really though, while you're still growing you should wait, bearing in mind they tend to get bigger as you get older. I'd say wait until you're at least in your 20's before making such a huge decision and bear in mind breast implants don't last forever; manufacturers say on average about 10yrs but for some women it's less and some it's more. Either way, you'll have to repeat the procedure every decade or so for the rest of your life. The earlier you have the procedure done the more hospital visits lie ahead for you and the more money it will cost you.... and the more scarring and the more risk of complications such as ruptures and infections each time. Remember that not all guys like big boobs and as I've stated before, they won't make you more loveable. Think about role models such as Keira Knightly who has rather a boyish figure; she's stunning and has boys drooling over her just the way she is.

"Breast implants don't last forever; manufacturers say on average about 10yrs"

"Nobody ever goes into a beauty salon and asks to look ridiculous"

FILLERS

It's true that full kissable lips are sexy. It's also true that lips pumped up with filler are not. In all the years of being a make-up artist I swear I can spot a fake mush a mile off! Please please pleeeeeeze think very hard before you go ahead with such an unpredictable and face changing procedure. Girls will convince each other that 'you can't tell' and that it looks 'totally natural' but it rarely does. I've worked with many models and actresses who flatly deny having had any work done when it's blatantly obvious to everyone else in the room that they have. It's not that they're trying to fool us particularly; it's more that they honestly don't think it looks unnatural and they can get away with it. The problem is that you soon get used to what you see in the mirror; your new fuller lips start to look 'normal' in your eyes so the next time you have a teeny bit more....and before you know it you look like a Furby.

When you start messing around with your face and have things injected, implanted or reduced you lose the character in it and start to look a bit alien; you can end up looking like Puffa Fish Barbie with hamster cheeks, sunken piggy eyes, a button nose and a mouth like a Bat Fish! Remember this, that nobody ever goes into a beauty salon and asks to look ridiculous. Nobody says 'please can you put way too much filler in my lips so that everybody will look at me and snigger behind my back'. It's a risk, every time, and that's before you've even considered the possibility of an allergic reaction!!

PERFECT POSTURE

LOOK SLIMMER, SEXIER AND MORE CONFIDENT

I can't tell you how important good posture is.....and why. I've always been tall....I was probably a tall baby if there is such a thing....but for sure I was always the tallest in class. I remember one summer our junior school teacher, Mr Mathews, taking us outside to do an experiment about the position of the sun throughout the year. He wanted to demonstrate this by using the length of shadows.... and guess whose shadow he chose? Yep, mine! He had me stand there in the middle of the playground at the same time once a week, in front of the whole class, while everyone watched as my shadow shot across the netball markings....someone measured it..... and it was marked on a graph. As the summer drew to a close and the sun got lower in the winter sky my

poor old shadow just grew and grew and grew....and the longer it got the more embarrassed I got. Not only was I tall but my shadow, my closest companion, freakishly tall; the graph now one magnificent curvy arc of pure height mockery. The two of us were.... well we were freaks!

The problem was that I didn't have that much self-confidence back then and so I thought my height was a negative thing. I wanted to be smaller so the natural thing to do was to stoop down a bit....try and hide a few of those unwanted shadowy inches. HOWEVER, I was lucky enough to have a wonderful mother who happened to be a model and who also ran a modelling school for 'poise and deportment' and it was her who made me understand about posture and how I had to "stand tall...be proud of my height". Every time we were out together she would demand "Shoulders back! Tummy innnn!" in a kind of singsong

military sort of way. I know if she hadn't I would have round shoulders by now and a sticky out belly but I don't, and throughout my life I've had dozens of people compliment me on my posture. In short, be proud of yourself – small or tall – you musn't hide away in an apologetic stance as people will perceive you as meek, weak and just a bit less attractive than you really are.

Good posture gives you an aura of ownership. Good posture tells people you're confident and makes people take notice of you; when you walk in a room you don't go unnoticed which is particularly handy when you either want that cute guy to spot you or more importantly that future employer! Good posture makes clothes look wayyy better but also it really does have health benefits. When you slouch your stomach muscles are relaxed and in time, unless you exercise, you'll have a pot belly – euch! You'll get neck and back ache and headaches too as well as poor digestion, depression and joint problems. You also look slimmer when you stand tall – it's stands to reason. So, the next time you catch yourself standing there or walking along with rounded shoulders and your tummy sticking out....just imagine staying that way because eventually you will. All together now, "Shoulders BACKKK, tummy INNNN!!!"

"I would have round shoulders by now and a sticky out belly"

MEL & TOM

BEN LUKE JOSH

BODY ART THINK BEFORE YOU INK!

I have a bit of a fascination with tattoos although I'd never have one – I think the simplicity of an unembellished skin is rather pure and beautiful. However, they're becoming so commonplace now it won't be long before the people who stand out the most will be the ones without any. Interesting concept huh!

It's a personal choice of course but personally I don't really get why you'd want an image on your skin to express who you are or what you're about; to literally wear your heart on your sleeve. I prefer to be more mysterious and wear my soul on the inside…and if people want to know more about me, they can ask!

Having said that, I do love looking at them; especially the really intricate arty ones. I've seen some really beautiful inkings in my time but even so, I don't know how you ever decide what to have! How can you know if you'll still like the same picture you like now in 50 years? I mean, if you look back ten years and try and remember what you loved then..... say, a boy band? Now imagine if you'd had them tattooed on your skin....would you still be happy and proud of your tat? I doubt it.

What if you fall in love with someone and, believing it'll be forever, you have their name tattooed on your arm. A couple of years pass and you realise that far from loving them....you actually can't bear the sight of them? You've gone off them in such a way your stomach churns at the very thought and yet, every time you catch yourself in the mirror there they are....their name glaring back at you mockingly. Of course, you could have the tattoo lasered off but have you any idea how painful that it? Or expensive? Oof – rather you than me! Unless it's the name of a family member or a pet who you actually will love forever I'd give it a miss.

If you're intent on having a tattoo though, and my blatant powers of persuasion haven't put you off (you have to be 18 by the way) you should definitely make sure the tattoo parlour is registered. Dirty needles can lead to life threatening infections such as septicaemia (blood poisoning), tetanus, hepatitis and HIV –

nobody wants that!

Now you need to make sure you've:

♥ Had a really good think about what to have. This will be with you forever.

♥ Considered what kind of message you're saying about you, because people will make judgements, like it or not.

♥ Had a really good think about where to have it. Do you want it on show the whole time or somewhere discrete. Think about when you're older and your style may have changed....you may get into wearing strappy dresses for instance, so ask yourself if the image you're having tattooed now will look good then, and there.

♥ Done your research and found the right tattooist for the kind of image you want. Each artist has their own style and skillset; some excel in portraiture and some in colour, others in tribal and others in delicate designs for example. Pick the right person for the job; it's not going to wash off!

♥ Seen some of the tattooist's work. Unless you've seen their work on someone you know, ask to look at photo's before committing to using them. A friend of mine had a star tattooed on his arm while we were in LA (it seemed simple enough) but the outline was all over the place and the colours looked like a 3yr old had done them....mind you the tattooist did look like

"That Tattoo looked great... last week".

ZZ Top (just...Google 'ZZ Top'...go on.... lol!!!!) We still laugh about it.

♥Had any foreign words or lettering properly translated or written correctly. Make sure you know exactly what the words say or how the letters should be drawn. A permanent spelling mistake or incorrect translation can make you a laughing stock should someone see it whose native language it is!

♥Checked that your chosen image doesn't have any hidden meanings. For instance, I read that some murderers have spider webs or teardrops to signify people they've killed. Ulp!

♥Sober! The worst time to get a tattoo is when you're drunk and even worse, in a foreign country. It's almost a given that you'll regret it and for Gawds sake don't ever do it for a bet.

Getting a tattoo is a personal choice, but if it's one you make, make it a good one!

PAUSE BEFORE YOU PIERCE!

Unlike tattooing there is no real age of consent for body piercing in the UK so long as a parent gives theirs. However, this changes somewhat when it comes to genital or nipple piercings (my eyes are watering at the thought of this) when you have to be at least 16 years old as the law deems it 'indecent assault'. Yikes.

The one advantage body piercings have over tattoos is that they don't have to be forever so they're not such a huge commitment. You must still do your research though and only go to a Heath & Safety registered salon as the risk of septicaemia (blood poisoning) and all those other hideous diseases (listed before with tattooing) is very real. If you decide you'd like a piercing and your parents are okay with it (if you're under the age of consent, that is) then it's recommended it's done using a needle instead of a piercing gun. According to my research, needles are more hygienic, less painful and less damaging to the skin tissue. Guns work by using the blunt end of the jewellery to pierce the flesh which is more traumatic to the skin and can complicate the healing process. Once you're bejewelled up, make sure you follow the advice for keeping the piercing clean to ward off any infections.

EXTREME PIERCINGS

When I think of the word tunnel I think of a long dark hole with a train coming out of it; I never imagined you could have one made of flesh!!! Alas, you can.....and if you're one of those people who fancy the idea of cultivating a massive gap in your lug hole I urge you to give it some proper thought before you do.

Unlike most regular piercings, which heal up once the jewellery is removed for long enough, a dangly loopy hole won't. Once the flesh has expanded beyond a certain point it will never spring back or close up, so if the time comes when you go off the idea of giant hula hoops framing either side of your face...... you'll be kinda stuffed. Well, there's always corrective surgery I suppose (which by the way is on the rapid increase which tells us something!!!!) but you'll have to find about 2 grand to cover it. It's not cheap.

"When you go off the idea of giant hula hoops framing either side of your face...... you'll be kinda stuffed"

If you still fancy the idea there's something else to consider. How about when you're going for job interviews? Biased and discriminative as it is, people with massive holes in their ears or facial tattoos often lose out on the work front (depending what line of work you're going in for of course). Yeah, I wish the world was more accepting of personal choice and expression but the reality is, it isn't. Not quite, and not yet.

PART 2 – INNER YOU

PERIODS – HOW TO COPE.

There are all sorts of fantastic things about being a girl. I LOOOOVE being one. If I had the choice to be reborn as a boy I'd flatly say no, "no thanks" I am very happy being a girl. We're awesome, we really are! I've always maintained that if women ruled the world there would hardly be any war and people wouldn't be starving in their millions. And why? Because women give birth.... their instinct is to nurture not to destroy, but while this is all very powerful stuff and self-congratulatory it does come with one big downside – periods!

The average age a girl starts her periods is 12 but for some it can be as young as 8 or as late as 15....either way it's all normal. For some girls periods are not such a big deal but for most of us they are one big fat pain in the butt.....or uterus if we're being precise. I hate periods. I have terrible periods. Biblical. Always have had. Some of my friends' only last about four days and are very light (lucky cows!) but if you're like me you'll suffer the full seven day leaky messy affair. That said, over the years I have worked out a system to help me cope and I'm going to share it with you now. First of all, the basics – which sanitary products do you want to use? Here's a list:

⭐ **Sanitary Pads** – thick slabs of cotton wool that stick onto your underwear and absorb your flow. They feel bulky and generally not very nice; you wouldn't want to wear a pair of tight leggings let's put it that way. They come in different absorbencies, sizes, thicknesses etc. it's a whole world of cotton woolly wonderment. Might be good to start out with before entering into tampon territory and always used by women post pregnancy when nothing can be inserted inside. Personally, I wouldn't touch them with a barge pole but sometimes needs must, I guess.

⭐ **Non-applicator tampons** – I don't quite understand how these little fellas are so popular. Basically they're tampons without an applicator which means you have to peel off the faffy cellophane wrapper then insert them using your finger....while grappling a bit of fiddly string so it doesn't get lost and so you can tug it out later on. Being a contortionist, double jointed, good at yoga or gymnastics may help here. Not so easy and let's face it....messy! Yuk!

⭐ **Tampons with applicators** – now we're talking. These tampons come with a smooth applicator and are dead easy and clean to insert so no scrubbing of hands afterwards and no acrobatics necessary to get them in, or out! Easy peasy. They come in different absorbencies; the thickest for heavy flow going down to the thinnest for light flow.

⭐ **Mooncup** – whaaaat??? What the heckingtons is that I hear you ask! This is a soft moulded silicone cup which is inserted inside and instead of it absorbing your period it captures it. Every few hours (they last longer than a tampon because they hold more fluid) you remove it, empty the contents, rinse and re-insert. Some women prefer this method; all you need is one Mooncup and it'll last you for years. In fact, on average a woman will use over 11,000 sanitary products in her lifetime so imagine how much money you'd save using this clever device. It's not for the feint hearted but if you're an eco-warrior princess (or have sensitive skin) this could be a great choice for you...once you get the hang of it.

⭐ **Panty Liners** – isn't 'Panty' a ridiculous word; it sounds so...wrong! Anyway, nevertheless these are great for either the last day of your period when a tampon is too much or for those who have heavy periods and need a bit of back up in the panty, ha!!!! Well, nothing's worse than being out and about and suddenly you feel a leak; your eyes practically pop out your head (always a giveaway) as sudden panic strikes and you adopt a strange 'my knees are suddenly glued together' walk to the Ladies. You have to have been there to understand that one girls!

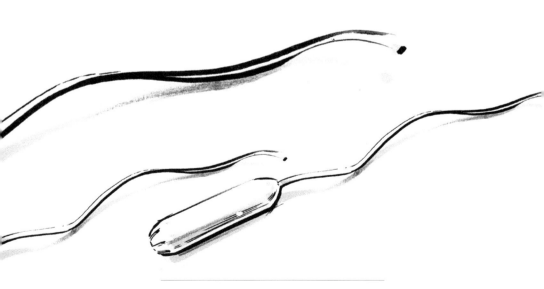

"*On average a woman will use over 11,000 sanitary products in her lifetime*"

As I said before my periods are heavy so here's what I do. I always have a stash of all the tampon absorbencies and for the first three days I'll use the highest absorbency along with a liner, and then say day four go to the next lowest absorbency. I do this until I'm down to the smallest lightest absorbency. It sounds like I'm buying a lot of tampons but they last four times as long as I only use a few of each for each period. You'll find that if you use a too high absorbency towards the end of your period they can feel uncomfortable to remove and insert as they (or you) will be too dry. You shouldn't use a tampon with too high absorbency for your flow anyway (information on this is always found in every pack of tampons) and you should change your tampon as needed, about every 4hrs but no more than a maximum of 8hrs. Once a tampon is inserted properly you literally cannot feel a thing; it's only felt if it's not inserted far enough inside in which case remove it and try again with another one. They also cannot 'get lost inside' as the string remains outside the body making it easy to remove. If however you somehow can't locate the string (which is highly unlikely) a quick trip to the doctor or nurse will sort it out.

As if monthly periods aren't enough they also come with an array of lovely (NOT) side effects such as:

☹ Period pains – deep aches in the abdomen and lower back (you may feel like you've been kicked by a small donkey) A nice comforting hot water bottle can help soothe the pain but if all else fails there are pain killers such as Feminax or simple Paracetamol which are most effective.

☹ Mood swings and tearfulness – you may become snappy or weepy or both the week leading up to your period but sadly this is pretty normal. Rotten isn't it!

☹ Bloating – try to avoid salty foods or alcohol (if you're old enough to drink it) as these will dehydrate you and make matters worse. Drink plenty of water to help flush toxins away and reduce puffiness.

☹ Bad hair days – my hair always goes flat and lank around my period so yours might too.

☹ Breakouts – girls often get spots leading up to their period; it's the hormones having a bit of a party...at your skin's expense. Try eating healthy non-fatty food and avoid sugary drinks and snacks as these will only add fuel to the fire.

☹ Overheating – I always know when my period's about to start because I always have a rubbish night's sleep the night before. Your body temperature rises slightly due to the fluctuation in hormones (yes, those again) leading to a restless night of broken sleep.

☹ Tender or fuller breasts – yep; all part and parcel of the joy of womanhood! Try wearing a soft support bra during these days for a bit of comfort.

Having said all that periods shouldn't stop you from getting on with your life, from doing sport (including swimming) or going out and having fun. Make sure you have an artillery of sanitary items with you (if you go clubbing take a pack of pocket tissues as you don't want to be caught out in the ladies with no toilet paper – imagine!) Also it might be a good idea to avoid those tight white skinny jeans for the first few days – red and white look great together.....but errrrr.....not like that!!!! Whatever, we've just got to get on with it girls so for goodness sake don't lose a week of your life curled up on the sofa when you don't have to.

HORMONES (OR HORMOANS)

Hormones are the little blighters which turn us into grumpy, weepy, snappy, over emotional lunatics the week before our periods. They're a very delicately balanced collection of chemical messengers, made in the ovaries, which have a huge effect on us. It takes only a tiny amount to cause big changes in cells or even the whole body, and too much or too little of a certain hormone can cause havoc. Certain factors other than your monthly period can mess with your hormone levels, like some medications and some forms of contraception. I can't tell you how many girls I've spoken to over the years who've suffered horrendous side effects from these.....including myself.

"It turned me into a crying emotional wreck it was AWFUL!"

It wasn't me, It was my Hormones!

I went on the Pill when I was 19 and it was brilliant; didn't feel any different but put on a little bit of weight. I later came off it for a few years then when I reached 30 I went back on it.....and oh dear me.....it turned me into a crying emotional wreck it was AWFUL! I came off it and voila, the fun loving easy going Jane was 'back in the room', phew. Similarly, dozens of friends and young girls I've chatted to about this have had the same sort of experiences with the Pill but also the Injection and the Implant too. Issy, now aged 20, told me how she felt out of control emotionally when she started taking the pill; that feeling when you KNOW you're being unreasonable or unjustifiably upset or weepy about something but you just can't stop it (exactly how I'd felt). If you have these sorts of feelings when you embark on a course of hormonal birth control you should go straight back to your doctor and ask for it to be changed; there may be other more suitable options so it really is a case of trial and error. A different pill could make the world of difference or simply having an implant removed and choosing something else. Just bear in mind it can take several months for your hormones to become balanced again so don't expect to feel all tickety boo the next day!

CONTRACEPTION – HOW TO AVOID PREGNANCY.

READY TO HAVE SEX?
OK – YOU'D BETTER READ THIS AND FAST!

For those who don't know, the age of consent when you're legally allowed to have sex in the UK is 16 years old (in other countries it ranges from 12 years old up to 20) but let's be honest…. there are many many girls who sleep with boys before then. We know this to be true because of the rate of underage teenage pregnancies, so, unless you fancy being pregnant at school ….or simply pregnant too young, you should decide what form of contraception you're going to use. Basically, as soon as you start your periods your body is 'ready' to make babies so be aware that even having sex once can lead to pregnancy. I must be clear I'm not a doctor but still it's good to know the basics about all the different birth control choices out there, and if you want to know more you can pop in to see your GP, a women's health centre or even explore more online. Here's a brief look at the different kinds of contraception available today:

☆ **The Rhythm Method** – sounds rather musical doesn't it. This is the riskiest method of all because it depends entirely on you knowing your menstrual cycle and your body to a 'T' and you'd need to have a very regular cycle….like clockwork. This is when you only have sex on the days you're not ovulating and avoid sex on all the other days. It doesn't allow for fluctuations in your cycle, but just as importantly doesn't protect you from STD's (Sexually Transmitted Diseases) either. I call it the 'Fingers Crossed Method' because you may as well just do that….then pray! It's worth remembering that some women are more fertile than others so while this may work for your friends it may not work for you. In my opinion it's the least reliable.

☆ **Caps and Diaphragms** – both these rather unattractive contraptions work in much the same way, the main difference being their size and shape. Diaphragms are surprisingly big, shockingly so, but once inside you can't feel them. The less popular Cap is much smaller and looks.....like a mutant mushroom, if I'm honest, and needs to be placed a little more accurately. They work by covering the cervix and are inserted before sex and removed no less than 6hrs afterwards and are reusable. Basically, you apply spermicide (which kills sperm) and place inside so that it covers the cervix to create a barrier between those pesky little swimmers and your lovely eggs. A doctor or nurse will have to measure you internally for one of these. According to the NHS website they are 92-96% effective providing they're used correctly. I must say they are rather messy to use and require practice and skill to get them in properly....you may find yourself breaking out in a mild sweat and cursing the gods until you get the hang of it and in truth, removing them is a little.... icky. However, if you fancy giving it a go it's worth remembering that if you gain or lose 7lbs or more you'll need to get measured again; if you lose weight on the outside you lose weight on the inside and vice versa...if you're thinner your diaphragm size increases! By the way, your partner shouldn't be able to feel it during sex. Again, you're not protected against STD's.

"In truth, removing them is a little.... icky"

⭐ **Condoms** – well they may not look all that attractive but really these flimsy little dudes work pretty brilliantly at preventing you getting pregnant; 98% effective! Condoms are the most sensible choice of contraception in many ways not least because they laugh in the face of STD's! Pretty much nothing is getting past one of these so you can rest assured you won't have any unwanted visitors taking up residence in your body!

⭐ **Female Condom** – yeah, I thought it was a joke too before I saw one! The idea of it.....it's just.....I mean.....I just can't look at one without chuckling to myself. I think these were invented for women who didn't feel they could rely on a man to use a condom and who wanted to take matters into their own hands. Apparently, they're 95% effective and like male condoms they will protect against STD's, but I think they look so darn un-sexy. By all means give one a go though; it's your call!

⭐ **Implant** – this is a small flexible tube which is inserted under the skin of your upper arm (by a doctor or nurse) which slowly releases the hormone Progestogen and lasts for up to 3yrs. It works by thickening the mucus at the entrance to the womb (the cervix) while making the womb lining thinner. These two factors make it almost impossible for an egg to get fertilized or indeed grow making the implant 99% effective. These have had some negative press recently so do your research carefully. You are not protected against STD's.

⭐ **Injection** – this works in pretty much the same way as an implant releasing Progestogen, except the injections tend to be either 8 weeks apart or 12 weeks apart depending which type you have. They're also 99% effective but also won't protect you against STD's.

⭐ **The Patch** – just like a Nicotine patch, this sticks onto the skin and releases a mixture of hormones which prevent the release of an egg (ovulation) as well as thinning the lining of the womb and thickening cervical mucus. 99% effective again but you'll still be at risk of contracting an STD. Once used always throw in the bin and not down the toilet. Frankly though I can't see why you'd want a 5cm anything stuck anywhere on your body...especially when there are other options, but I do think it's great there are so many choices out there.

⭐ **Coils** – there are two types of coil; an IUD and an IUS. Contrary to the name 'Coil' (I can't help but think of a massive rusty old coil inside a car engine!) there's nothing curly or coily about them – quite the opposite. They're both small flat 'T' shaped devices which are inserted through the cervix into the womb by a trained doctor or nurse. Once inside you can't feel them at all although they can feel uncomfortable during insertion so you might want to take pain killers an hour beforehand just in case. The IUD is similar to the IUS but works in a different way. Instead of releasing the hormone progestogen like the IUS, the IUD releases copper. Copper changes the make-up of the fluids in the womb and fallopian tubes, stopping sperm surviving there. Significantly, an IUD lasts for up to 10 years while an IUS needs to be replaced after 5 years and both are 99% effective. While all this sounds fantastic there can be all sorts of side effects and you are still at risk of STD's.

⭐ **The Pill** – there's a choice of the Combined Pill (using oestrogen and progestogen) which you take for 21 days then break for 7, and the Progestogen Only Pill which you take every day without a break. There are dozens of different pills available but only a doctor should prescribe which one is best suited to your personally, since there are many factors which need to be considered in order to make them safe. Both are 99% effective but as with all hormonal forms of contraception come with a rather long list of possible side effects....and no you've guessed it....you're not protected against STD's.

"Don't go messing with those hormones and your precious body!"

☆ **The Ring** – this is a small soft plastic ring which once inserted stays inside for 21 days, after which it's removed and thrown in the bin (not the toilet; we don't want those hormones getting into our water system), then after 7 days you simply insert another. It releases the hormones progestogen and oestrogen like the Combined Pill but this way you don't have to remember to take it every day.

☆ **The Morning After Pill**.....this is known as 'Emergency Contraception' and should be taken if your usual method of contraception has failed eg. the condom broke or you forgot to take your birth control pill. The M.A.P should be taken within 3 to 5 days after intercourse depending on which pill you are given but be aware there can be side effects such as abdominal pain and headaches etc, and if taken too often can disrupt your menstrual cycle too. So, if you don't think you need to use contraception 'because there's always the morning after pill' think again; don't go messing with those hormones and your precious body!

Before I close this chapter on contraception there's something you need to know about boys. Often before a guy fully ejaculates he will produce fluid known as 'pre-cum' ('pre-ejaculate' if we're being all clinical about it) and this, in most cases, contains sperm. So, if you're fooling around with no intention of penetrative sex and your genitals come into contact with theirs, even without going the whole way, there's still a risk of getting pregnant if this gets anywhere near inside you!!!

STD'S – SEXUALLY TRANSMITTED DISEASES

Before you decide which option appeals to you the most remember that the OHHHHHNLY contraceptive device which protects against sexually transmitted diseases is the CONDOM! (Female or otherwise - heheeee!) A condom acts as a barrier to prevent all types of body fluids and germs from coming into contact with your body.... NO OTHER BIRTH CONTROL DOES THIS!!!!! Sorry, did I shout then? Well, the problem is that often some STD's show no symptoms at all until much later so there's no way of knowing if your partner has contracted something..... but equally horrifying is that you won't know if YOU have either! For instance, Chlamydia can be symptom free for a few weeks or even months, and if left undetected and untreated can spread to the womb causing PID (Pelvic Inflammatory Disease) which in turn can lead to infertility, ectopic pregnancy or miscarriage. Crikey – scary stuff (and you thought simply NOT getting pregnant was the issue!)

While on the topic of condoms, can I just say that if someone you're about to have shenanigans with refuses to use a condom he may not be the kind of person you should be getting naked with. Given that we've just established that STD's can be symptom free, he could well be carrying something.....perhaps his last girlfriend had something she wasn't aware of.....and perhaps her ex-boyfriend had something.....and his ex.....and so it goes on. If you look at it that way a condom starts to really make sense.

If you have had sexual contact with someone and have developed any unusual symptoms down below such as itching, strange coloured or odd smelling discharge or any lumps bumps or blisters, you must get yourself to your doctors (or book an appointment at your nearest sexual health clinic) to have it checked out asap. It's always better to play it safe, and usually a course of antibiotics will sort things out so don't fret! While most STD's are not life-threatening some have very serious consequences and in the case

"They don't know you and they're not judging you – they just want to help you"

of HIV can prove fatal. There's a great saying 'don't die of embarrassment', so push those thoughts aside and make that call. The receptionists, doctors and nurses at these special clinics do this every single day; they don't know you and they're not judging you – they just want to help you get well and try to prevent the spread of these kinds of diseases.

THE NHS WEBSITE IS A GREAT PLACE TO GET MORE DETAILED INFORMATION ABOUT STD'S: NHS.UK

PREGNANCY – YOU THINK YOU MIGHT BE PREGNANT?

If you've had penetrative sex (or if you and your boyfriend's genitals have come into contact) and your period is late, you might be pregnant. Here are some common symptoms:

THE TELLTALE SIGNS

1 YOUR PERIOD IS LATE.

2 **YOUR PERIOD IS LIGHTER THAN NORMAL.**

3 YOUR BREASTS ARE TENDER AND LARGER THAN USUAL.

4 **YOUR NIPPLES ARE VERY SENSITIVE TO TOUCH.**

5 YOU FEEL SICK OR START VOMITING; MORNING SICKNESS CAN HAPPEN ANY TIME DAY OR NIGHT SO DON'T BE FOOLED.

6 **YOU FEEL PARTICULARLY TIRED.**

7 YOU START PEEING A LOT.

8 **YOU STOP POOING A LOT (AKA CONSTIPATION!).**

9 YOU BECOME OVERSENSITIVE TO TASTES AND SMELLS.

You may not get all of these, but if your periods have stopped and you get any of these other symptoms too you MUST get yourself a pregnancy test as soon as possible. Just pop to your nearest chemist where you can buy one over the counter....there is NO NEED TO BE EMBARRASSED!!!! I promise you that you're not being judged; the person who serves you honestly doesn't give a toss about you or your sex life – you're just another customer in their busy day, that's all. Wait until the next morning when your urine is the most concentrated and pee on the stick (usually a few seconds) then wait. Follow the instructions on the box to see how to read the indicator; some literally spell it out saying 'Pregnant' or 'Not pregnant' and some will even tell you how many weeks. Presuming that you'd rather not be pregnant, here's what to do next if ....

IT'S NEGATIVE

After you've done a little dance of joy and high fived yourself you still need to wait and see if your period comes, as it's possible you've done the test too early. Hopefully it'll come a day or so later and you can take it as a lesson learned. If, however, nothing's happening say two weeks later – no period – do another test. If it still reads 'Negative'

but you're still getting other symptoms you should go and see your doctor JUST TO BE SURE. Again, you don't need to feel embarrassed; doctors much prefer you come to them early while you have options rather than late when you have none! If your periods stop it could be an indicator of an undetected illness or even just stress; for instance, having exams or job interviews can put a lot of strain on our finely tuned bodies and sometimes this can interrupt your menstrual cycle.

IT'S POSITIVE

If the test reads positive it is not the end of the world. I know what it's like when you're scared you might be pregnant (I think every sexually active girl has had moments like this) and you suddenly start to panic about telling your parents; you think your world is about to fall apart. The thing is IF you are indeed pregnant you CANNOT ignore it and you MUST TELL SOMEONE. The embryo inside you will continue to grow with every day that passes, like it or not, and the sooner you share your condition with someone you trust (preferably your parents), the better. Understandably they're going to be upset since they no doubt have high hopes for you in life; their vision of you conquering the world one day with a baby attached to your hip doesn't really gel. They might

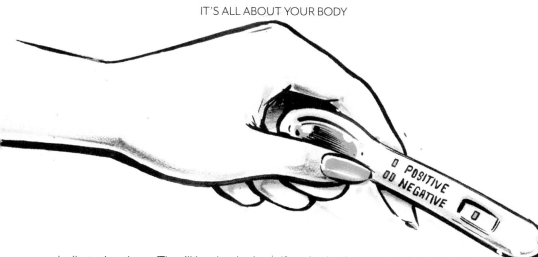

go ballistic. Let them. They'll be shocked and disappointed and full of questions but mainly they will be a bit scared and a lot worried...about you. Once the initial news sinks in and they've calmed down they will no doubt become your greatest allies and supporters because they love you ....they will help you every step of the way whichever decision you decide to make. Please understand you should not go through this alone. If you don't have a great relationship with your mum or dad (or maybe they're no longer in your life) you still need to seek advice from someone older who you trust. Everything will be ok; you must believe me.....time will pass and all will be well.

> "Being pregnant doesn't make you a bad person, a slut, a disappointment"

If you've had sex under the legal age limit you may be scared to tell someone you're pregnant in case you get into trouble (just so you know, you're not going to get arrested) If this is the case and it's preventing you from telling an adult I really really urge you that you do. The one and only important person here is you and your health and wellbeing; it's first and foremost. Unwanted teenage pregnancies happen – fact. You're not the first and you won't be the last. Being pregnant doesn't make you a bad person, a slut, a disappointment....it doesn't mean anything other than a sperm fertilized an egg. That's what humans are put on the earth for...to procreate. All you've done is got your timing wrong and been careless. Now dry your tears, be strong, and go and get some help and support.

I FOUND THIS GREAT WEBSITE JUST FOR TEENS ANSWERING ALL YOUR QUESTIONS ABOUT SEX:SEXETC.ORG OR SCARLETEEN.COM

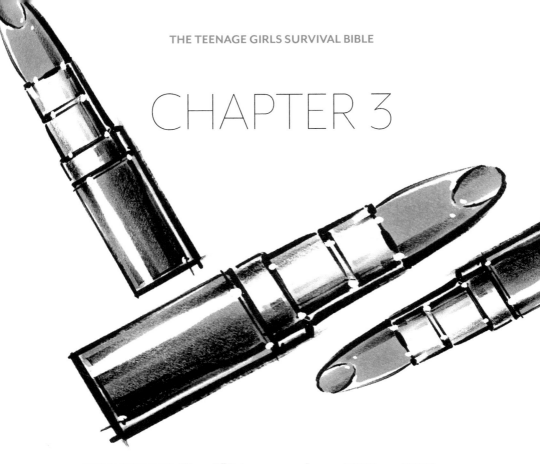

CHAPTER 3

IT'S ALL ABOUT Face

THE MAGIC OF
MAKE-UP

IF YOU'RE A MAKE-UP lover you'll understand how confusing and overwhelming it is when you go out to buy the stuff; there's so much choice!!!!! Even when you've bought it there's the whole other issue of how to apply it. I'm going to break it down for you to help you make the right choices and make sure you don't end up looking like a drag queen.

TINTED MOISTURISERS, BB'S AND CC'S

If you're fortunate enough to have good skin there's no need to mask it with heavy foundation, especially at your age when you're wrinkle and sun damage free! One of these babies should do the trick nicely, and seeing as they're only lightly pigmented it's much easier to colour match with your skin:

⭐ **Tinted Moisturiser** – imagine mixing face cream with foundation et voila; tinted moisturiser! Apply all over the face with your fingers then use concealer for under eye circles or blemishes. These tend to have a dewy finish and are best suited to normal/dry skins. To be honest, you could easily mix a liquid foundation with your favourite moisturiser and get the same effect (a trick I've used for years on my clients!)

⭐ **BB creams** – the letters stand for 'beauty balm' or 'blemish balm' and are similar in look and feel to tinted moisturisers but with added benefits. No two BB Creams are alike depending on the brand, so you'll need to find one which caters to your needs, but generally they offer a selection of ingredients which claim to prime, reduce redness, minimise fine lines, moisturise, cover, brighten

PREPPING THE SKIN

Before you even think about applying a dot of make-up on your face you must make sure your skin is properly prepped! First apply the correct moisturiser for your skin type whether it's normal, dry, oily or combination. This will help your base go on more evenly, but always give it a few minutes to absorb before applying anything else. At this stage, you might want to use a Primer. Primers are designed to create a smoother surface for your foundation and help prolong its wear, add radiance or help mattify your skin depending which one you choose. You only need use a small amount and rather than rub it in you lightly smooth it over the surface instead. Having said that you don't necessarily need a primer and most make-up artists will agree they seldom use them unless their client's skin needs some extra help.

and protect against the sun. Having said that it's still recommended you use a moisturiser first (especially if you have dry skin) and seeing as the finish is 'natural' you may need concealer for any blemishes or under eye circles too....and maybe powder if the finish is too dewy for your liking. Phew.

⭐ **CC creams** – these are a variation of BB creams but mean 'Colour Correcting' as they also contain pigments to help reduce redness or sallowness (when your skin looks yellowy). Use them in the same way as BB's. They can be worn under foundation like a primer.

FOUNDATION

If none of the above are packing enough punch you'll need to use a foundation. Getting it right is the cornerstone of great make-up, and if the colour or formula is wrong you'll be fighting a losing battle trying to get the rest of your make-up to look any good.

Working out which sort of foundation to buy depends on four main things; the kind of skin you have (eg. oily, normal or dry), the shade of your skin, the kind of coverage you need and the finish you prefer. It might take a bit of trial and error but once you've found your match the rest will be plain sailing.

Here are my top tips:

💜 Dry or flaky skins like a liquid or creamy base. Oil free formulas or anything too powdery will look too flat and lifeless and draw attention to any little parched patches.

💜 Oily skins prefer something with staying power so nothing too rich or greasy feeling. They like oil free formulas, powder foundation compacts, loose mineral foundation or long wear bases which dry to a nice velvety finish.

💜 Normal skins like pretty much anything – lucky you!

💜 Your base should match your skin tone perfectly. Light skins tend to have either a yellow, pink or neutral undertone while dark skins tend to have yellow, red, or blue (and even ash!). It's an important factor to get right and can be difficult to work out. I recommend going to a store with trained staff who can offer advice and guide you towards your perfect shade. Don't be shy to ask...it's what they're there for and they love to help!

💜 The perfect shade should 'disappear' on your skin when you look in the mirror; it should be seamless with your own skin colour.

💜 Before splashing the cash on a foundation it's better you try it for a day to see how it truly looks, performs and lasts on your face. Always ask for a sample to take home but in case you can't get one, take some little empty pots of your own and ask for a few drops to be dispensed in them from the Testers. This can save some costly mistakes!

♥ Shop lighting is never geared towards the finer points of make-up shopping, so when trying out a foundation in store it's best to pop outside into the natural daylight and have a proper look in a hand mirror. Who cares if people stare; you want to choose the right shade, right? Right!

♥ Not all foundations stay colour true. If you have particularly oily skin they can oxidise and change colour quite dramatically throughout the day. This occurs mainly on very pale skin where the foundation can turn orange, and on darker skins where the colour just goes much deeper. If this happens try changing your foundation, your moisturiser or use an oil control primer underneath.

♥ Applying foundation with a brush or sponge will help give a lovely even finish, but if you struggle with acne it's better to apply with your fingers as bacteria can lurk on these tools.

♥ If you have a suntan your usual foundation will be too pale so you'll need a darker shade to match your darker skin. As your tan fades you can start blending it with a mix of your usual paler shade until it returns to normal. Mix on your hand not your face!

#TIP

Instead of buying a mattifying primer I learned a brilliant tip from a couple of gorgeous backing singers I know; thanks Adetoun and Zee!. They simply sweep talc all over their faces before applying foundation, and when they come off that hot sweaty stage two hours later their make-up still looks banging!

♥ If you tan your body but leave your face out of the sun your face will be paler than your body (yeah, we got that!) SO, don't make the mistake of continuing with your everyday base as you'll end up with what I call 'floating face' (where your pale face floats above your bronzed body) Instead use a base in the same shade as your tan and MATCH it to the rest of you!! Alternatively use fake tan on your face so you're seamlessly the same colour.

♥ Loose mineral foundation is especially great for sensitive skins and problem oily skins as they're made from pure minerals. You can build them up for great coverage but always apply with a kabuki brush in a swirling motion as you buff into the skin. If you have dry skin make sure you moisturise well beforehand and allow it to sink in, or, try a liquid mineral base instead.

♥ It's not necessarily the case that you'll find your exact shade in every cosmetic brand, especially if you have an olive to dark skin where there are so many slight variants. Shop around and don't be pushed into a purchase you're not sure about!

♥ Mix a little liquid or loose mineral highlighter into your base for a more glowy alternative!

CONCEALER

I've covered these in Chapter 2, part 1, where I've explained how to go about dealing with problem skin. However, concealers are also there to simply give added coverage to any areas which need a little extra help and can be used alone or on top of foundation on areas that need extra coverage such as under the eyes.

Here are some general concealer rules:

♥ Use highly pigmented concealers to hide blemishes; they have a thicker consistency than those used under the eyes and provide extra coverage. These come in palettes, sticks or pencils.

♥ Creamy liquid concealers which come in a tube with a wand tend to be best for under the eyes as they have a medium consistency and won't look cakey.

♥ Illuminating concealer pens don't actually 'conceal' due to their sheerness but work by bouncing light off the skin giving a radiant glow. They're best applied under the eyes, along the top of cheekbones, on the brow bone, corners of the eyes, down the centre of the nose and the cupids bow. Apply sparingly over foundation or over regular concealer. Never use these to hide spots or blemishes.

♥ Concealer should match your skin exactly when covering any sort of blemish. However, when used with foundation under the eyes you could go a fraction lighter for a subtle bit of extra brightness.

♥ It's often just the small inner triangle of skin under the eye which needs brightening; the bit under the tear duct. Tip your head down and look up into the mirror to help make this area more visible and apply concealer just there instead of the whole way under the eye.

♥ Applying a little creamy liquid concealer in a slightly lighter shade on the eyelids and inner corners of the eyes will instantly brighten them...and while you're there pop a little on the brow bone under your eyebrows too.

♥ Always apply your concealer after your liquid or cream foundation. The foundation will provide some coverage meaning you'll need to use less concealer thereby reducing the amount of make-up on your face. Less is more! However, when using powder foundation always apply concealer and any colour correctors first.

Sometimes a regular flesh toned concealer just isn't enough to combat particularly stubborn under eye circles or marks on the face so you need to learn about colour correcting. This guide will help you choose what shade to use to help cancel out or neutralise any offending areas:

☆ Dark circles which have a blue undertone need an **ORANGE** toned concealer which cancels out blue shadows. It can also be used to lighten any dark areas on darker skins. Once applied, go over this with a concealer or foundation that matches your skin tone.

☆ Dark circles with a blue/purple undertone require more of a **PEACH OR SALMON** toned concealer. Use on any blue toned bruises or dark spots too.

☆ Under eye circles which appear more purple need a **YELLOW** based concealer. This also works on black toned bruises.

☆ **GREEN** concealers or colour correctors cancel out redness, so if you have high colouring, rosacea, red patches or pink toned scars try this under your foundation making sure you pat, stipple or press the foundation over the area you've corrected.

☆ **LILAC** concealers bring life to a yellowy 'sallow' skin and they also cancel out any yellow toned bruises.

POWDER

I don't use powder very often on my clients as I prefer the skin to have a slight natural sheen to it, but sometimes it's necessary. Powder is used to mattify the skin (with or without foundation) and set make-up in place.

Here are my powder pointers:

Choose a powder in the same shade as your skin or foundation.

Generally speaking, a yellow toned powder will look neutral on most skin tones unless you're super fair and have a pale, pinky undertone to your skin. Use a more neutral or colourless shade.

Thanks to HD TV and Film the newest formulations of powder are super sheer and almost invisible...because they have to be!

Dark skin tones need warm toned powder; anything ranging from yellow to brown. Pale cool toned powders will make the skin look ashy and drain the life out of you!

Beware of shimmery powders on light skins which can look very shiny.

Dark skins look great with shimmery powders such as golden or rusty bronzers which help bring the skin to life.

Never swipe powder over your foundation with a powder puff. Instead, press and roll the puff onto your skin then dust off any excess with a large fluffy brush.

Pressed powders are best for when you're on the move and loose powders should stay at home; they're bulky and prone to spillage.

You don't always need to powder the whole face! Try applying just on the T Zone which tends to be more oily eg. the forehead, sides of the nostrils, either side next to the nose, chin and upper lip.

Powdering the eyelids before applying eye shadow will help give a more even finish. This area tends to be oily leading to patchiness.

BRONZER

Girls seem to be obsessed with bronzer but honestly, I don't use it that much in my kit. If a client's face is too pale (paler then the rest of her I mean) I warm it up with foundation or tinted moisturiser instead as it looks more natural. However, you can make bronzer look great if you know how and where to apply it properly.

Bronzer's not really supposed to be applied all over your entire face; this will look rather bizarre especially if your neck is pale - you'll end up looking like a giant chocolate button lollypop. Nope, you need to be a lot more strategic than that! If you think how your face tans naturally, the places which catch the sun the most (known as 'the high points') are around the hairline and temples, bridge of the nose, top of the cheekbones and the chin. Use bronzer to mimic this by applying in the same places using a medium sized fluffy brush starting with a little at a time and building up where necessary. You'll also need to apply a little on the neck too to make sure it's the same colour as the rest of your face.

Here are my tan-trick tips:

💜 Choose a bronzer to complement your skin tone.

💜 Make sure any moisturiser has been properly absorbed first and if foundation is applied, make sure it sets or give it a tickle of powder before bronzing. This prevents any potential patchiness.

💜 If you have fair skin opt for a bronzer which isn't too sparkly or you'll look like a disco mirror ball with hair.

💜 Dark skins look gorgeous with the more shimmery bronzers but make sure you choose a warm gold or deep bronze shade and you'll look fantastic.

💜 Make sure you blend well so there are no defined edges.

💜 Using a dense thick brush will distribute far too much product as will a small flat brush (such as those found in some compacts) Use a larger fluffy brush for best results.

💜 Try also sweeping a little bronzer along the jawline to frame the face or even over the eyelids for a touch of colour.

💜 Sweeping highlighter along the tops of the cheekbones looks gorgeous with bronzer to help give extra luminosity.

💜 A touch of coral/peach/pink blusher works well with bronzer for that 'just left the beach' healthy bloom.

💜 Once you've completed your masterpiece spritz your face with a fixing mist. Lots of brands do these now to ensure your skin doesn't look at all powdery while helping bind the makeup for longer wear.

BLUSHER

One of my favourite products is blusher as it brings the face to life. It's available in several formulas such as powder, cream, gel and liquid but you need to know these application tips:

♥ Cream blusher should be worn alone or on TOP of your cream/liquid foundation. Never apply it on top of powder foundation as it will drag and look patchy.

♥ Liquid blusher should be applied in the same way as cream blusher.

♥ Apply creams and liquids with either your fingers, a mini beauty blender or a stipple brush and blend well.

♥ Gel blushers and those very thin watery blushers which look like red ink are pretty tricky to apply. I always find the pigment settles into the pores leaving little colour elsewhere. I'd give these a wide berth if I were you!

♥ Powder blusher should be applied onto a matte base such as powder foundation or foundation which has been powdered. A sticky surface will result in patchiness and make it impossible to blend.

♥ Blusher is there to give the illusion of healthy rosy cheeks so think about where you're applying it. Use it on the apples of the cheeks and blend outwards towards the ear but not touching the ear. If you don't naturally blush there, don't put it there!

♥ Once you've applied a cream blush you can sweep a little powder over the top to help set it....although you'll lose the dewy glow, of course.

♥ Cream blushers often work well on the lips too for a soft stain of matching colour which can look lovely and effortless.

♥ Apply powder blush with a medium sized tapered or rounded fluffy brush starting with a little at a time and buff outwards in circular motions. Avoid using the little brushes that often come in the compact as they're too small and firm for the job; you'll end up with unsightly stripes!

♥ Don't use blush to contour your face; use a matte contouring shade instead.

CONTOURING & HIGHLIGHTING

Make-up artists have been shaping faces using this technique for decades but it's only recently it's become a standard step in any girl's make-up routine. The idea of contouring and highlighting is to add shape, shade, and light to the face to give the illusion of more pronounced features. It can change the way a face looks when it's done properly and subtly; the key is to BLEND!!

Check out my face chart (opposite) to demonstrate how it works:

GREY – apply your contour shade here. This should be a few shades darker than your skin tone and is used to sculpt and minimise areas of the face. Apply under the cheekbones, around the hairline and jawline, and for a slimmer looking nose apply down the sides.

WHITE – this is your highlight colour which makes features more prominent. Apply above the centre of the brows, top of the cheekbones, bridge of the nose and centre of the chin.

PINK – this is your blusher shade which should sit between the contour shade and the highlighter.

While oval and heart shaped faces need little extra help, you might want to try these specific techniques if you have a particularly long, round or square shaped face:

LONG: Contour along the top of the hairline, under the tip of the nose, under the cheekbones and tip of the chin to help shorten the face. Highlight along the top of the cheekbones to the hairline. Apply everything in a horizontal direction including your blush shade.

ROUND: Contour down the sides of the face and temples and under the cheek bones in a downward direction to lengthen the face. Blend the highlighter towards the top of the hairline, down the centre of the nose and the centre of the chin, but don't take it too near the hairline when sweeping along the tops of your cheekbones. Apply everything in a vertical direction including your blush shade.

SQUARE: Contour the upper right and left side of the forehead and the outer edges of the jawline to soften the 'corners' of the face. Highlight along the cheekbones curling up towards the temples and mimic this shape with your blush shade. Apply everything in a curvy shape.

Using the right brushes is essential. Angled medium sized brushes are great for contouring under the cheekbones, tip of chin and hairline. A small flat brush is best to contour the sides of the nose and a small oval brush for the eye socket.

A fluffy small brush is great for highlighting the top of cheekbones, above the brow and chin. A small flat brush is best used for the cupids bow, under the brow and bridge of the nose.

You can highlight using a shimmery (not glittery!) powder, a cream or liquid, a highlighting pen or use a light shade concealer.

Contour powder should be almost matte and if you have light skin use a neutral cool hue; if they're too orangey it can look like badly placed blusher!

Create the illusion of fuller lips by placing a little highlighter to the top of the cupids bow.

Make your eyes sparkle by dabbing a touch of highlighter to the inner corners of the eyes and under the brow bone too.

If using a Beauty Blender, make sure you dampen it first then squeeze out any excess water. Use the big rounded end all over the face and the smaller pointy end for those tricky little nooks.

Be very careful when shading your nose as it's it's very easy to make it look wider than it really is. If you're trying to slim it down, make sure the contouring down the sides blends far enough towards the bridge, leaving a narrow strip for the highlighter. Also, if your contouring isn't straight, you can inadvertently make your nose look wonky....or broken even!

Look out for 'contour and highlight' palettes which save space and money.

Highlight shades should create a sheen on the skin without necessarily adding colour. If you're very fair, anything more than an ivory tone will look like your blusher has gone AWOL! Fair skins suit ivory or pale gold shades, dark skins look awesome with gold tones and very dark skins with pink tones.

If you have very dry skin or have eczema in areas you'd like to highlight choose a cream or liquid formula as shimmery powders will exaggerate any dry areas.

If you prefer a more natural look then skip the contouring and just highlight the top of the cheekbones which looks gorgeous no matter what!

Finally, did I say the word 'blend'? Yes, I know I did...but really, it's an absolutely vital part of contouring and highlighting, and unless you do it properly you'll look a little freakish. Blend blend BLEND!!!!!

EYE SHADOW

There are a gazillion tutorials on YouTube showing a million different ways to wear eye shadow; the combinations are endless. So, instead of covering 'looks' (which would take for-evvvvv-errrrrr) how about we focus on tips instead!

♥ When buying those chubby style eye shadow pencils make sure they dry when tested on the back of the hand. If they stay creamy after a couple of minutes and smudge when rubbed, they'll crease like crazy on your eyes.

♥ Matte powders are harder to blend than shimmery ones so if you're having trouble with them try to find one in a similar shade but with a slight bit of sheen.

♥ Use the correct brush for the job. A firm flat brush is best for applying dense colour all over the lid and a longer more diamond shape brush is best for applying colour into the sockets. Use a fluffy brush to blend the colours together and to ensure the colour 'melts' away at the edges.

♥ The key to great eye shadow is all in the blending so make sure the colours are seamless.

♥ If you find your eye shadow falls and creates a right old mess under the eyes during application, try applying your foundation on the lower part of your face afterwards. You can then clean any debris off, apply the rest of your base and voila – immaculate looking skin!

♥ If you want to invest in some eye shadows I advise starting out with a palette of neutrals or 'earth tones' as you'll never go wrong.

♥ When using an eye shadow quad here's a general guide: Use the lightest colour under your brow, the second lightest on the lid, the next darkest colour in the socket (or crease) and the darkest on the outer corner blending into the crease.

♥ When creating a smoky eye apply a dark shade all over the eye lid but make sure that when you open your eyes you can see the colour above the crease; this is essential! Take the colour underneath the eye too making sure it joins up at the outer corner. Blend the edges using a slightly lighter shade of shadow then use a neutral shade under the brow bone.

♥ Work out what eye shape you have then search out every trick there is for that shape.

♥ Eye shadow usually looks best when a bit of eye liner is applied to the lash line to help frame the eyes. Make this your darkest shade.

♥ Always apply mascara AFTER eye shadow to prevent what I call 'dirty lashes'.....when eye shadow falls onto the lashes and coats them with a film of powdery dust.

EYELINER

Oh, how I love a good eyeliner; it makes such a difference to the eyes! Decide what look you're going for and Line-Up for my tips:

♥ Pencils can be used to create a precise line but can be tricky to achieve especially if they're too soft. If so, go over the pencil with a very small brush dipped into a matching eye shadow to give a clean edge.

♥ Gel pencils are the best! They're rich in pigment and once dry they set beautifully for long lasting wear. Great for use along the lash line as well as the waterline.

♥ Soft kohl pencils smudge....so avoid these if it's precision you're after!

♥ Keep your pencils sharpened for clean professional results and ease of application.

♥ Bright coloured pencils can look grrrreat worn on the waterline when creating a smoky eye. They also look FAB worn boldly under the eye with neutral tones on the rest of the face.

♥ Stippling black or brown pencil into the roots of the lashes makes your lashes look thicker. There's also a technique called 'tight-lining' where you run your eye pencil under the inner rim of your upper lashes, but make sure you use a waterproof or gel type pencil.

♥ Try precision lining with a gel eyeliner. Apply using a small, short firm brush to create anything from a fine line to a fabulous feline flick.

♥ If you can't be bothered with a brush and a pot of gel then opt for a pen style liner which are easy to use and come with varying lengths and tips; some are finer than others so find one you like.

♥ Liquid eyeliner is the trickiest of all to apply due to its consistency and drying time. There's usually a very fine brush attached to the lid allowing for very fine detail and the finish, once dried, is usually more shiny than other kinds of liner.

♥ After applying gel or liquid liner run your finger along the tips of your lashes to clean off any blobs which may ruin the rest of your make-up.

♥ You need a steady hand to apply these sorts of liners so either support your elbow with your free hand or rest it on a solid surface. You'll then be able to pivot your arm freely for smooth confident application.

♥ If you have small eyes don't use dark eye pencil on the waterline as this will make your eyes look even smaller. Instead try a flesh tone pencil which will open them up.

♥ If you have eyes which pop out a bit or the lower lid droops, it's worth trying dark eye pencil on the waterline as this reduces the amount of space between the lashes.... making the eyes appear a little smaller.

MASCARA

Mascara has to be my 'desert island essential' as it really frames the eyes. However, before you get started you might want to give your lashes a bit of extra curl with an eyelash curler; you'll be amazed at the difference it makes. Here's how to be utterly Lashtastic:

♥ ALWAYS use lash curlers on CLEAN lashes. Used after mascara the curler will stick to the hair, and when you release the grip you'll either break the lashes off or pull some out. Ouch...and not a good look! You don't want 'lash mange' do ya!

♥ Ease the curler over your lashes and get it as near to the roots as possible. Gently squeeze, and when you're sure you haven't trapped any skin, apply more pressure and hold for about two seconds. Release your grip then move the curler a tiny bit further along the lashes and squeeze firmly again. Repeat along to the end of the lash and tadaahhh, lovely curvy lashes!

Now for the fun bit; the mascara!

♥ Apply mascara from root to tip. Wiggle the wand from side to side at the base of the lashes to really get the colour in there, then pull the wand through the length of the lash. This is coat one. Repeat a few times then swap to the other eye then, before the mascara has dried on the first eye, go back and add another coat. If you allow the first coat to dry you'll have a problem getting the second one on smoothly.

♥ Once the top lashes are dry, bring your chin down and look up into the mirror which will lift the lower lashes away from the skin. Now apply one coat of mascara.

♥ Remove any clumps by using a clean spiral brush or lash comb. If you have weedy lower lashes don't draw attention to them by applying mascara onto the few you have. Instead use a little eye shadow under the eye to help frame them.

♥ If you're prone to very watery eyes or

find your out-of-control hormones drive you to tears all too often, I strongly advise using a waterproof formula! Nothing worse than a girl with sooty black rivers running down her face! You'll need an oil based eye make-up remover to get it off, then remove any residue with a bit of toner on a cotton wool pad.

♥ Smudge proof mascara will withstand a minimal amount of moisture but having a good old cry or doing a few lengths of the swimming pool will only end in panda eyes. On the positive side, they do come off with any sort of eye make-up remover.

♥ If you find your mascara always smudges under your eyes don't apply it to the tips of the lower lashes or, once you've applied it gently swipe your finger along the edges to make sure there's nothing there to smudge!

♥ I'm a massive fan of black mascara but if you're very fair or a redhead and feel it's too dramatic, choose dark brown. Coloured mascara is fun but for everyday it doesn't pack the same punch.

♥ Despite what you're told, just because a mascara wand is curved it will not make your eye lashes curl. It's like brushing your hair with a round brush; it's not going to make it curly!!

♥ Keep it simple when choosing a mascara and choose one with a straight brush with a pointy end (I favour the plastic wand type myself for delivery of product and lash separation) Gimmicky shaped brushes are just another way of seducing you into buying another mascara; us make-up artists find this trickery rather amusing!

♥ Don't pump the mascara wand in and out the tube to try and get more product on the brush; this only pumps air in which dries out the mascara. Instead, swirl the brush inside the tube.

♥ Some lash products that claim to encourage the growth of your lashes actually DO work! Some work better than others so do your research as they can be pricy!

"CHOOSE A GUY WHO RUINS YOUR LIPSTICK, NOT YOUR MASCARA"

♥ If your lashes are sparse try using individual false lashes to fill in the gaps. Use a good glue such as Duo Lash and buy the 'Short' ones as the Medium are usually just to long. In fact, I use these on my clients all the time but put them along the whole length of the eye; they give the most natural finish and look awesome especially when finished off with a swipe of mascara.

For extra glamorama why not experiment with strip lashes! Strip lashes with few hairs make little difference to your eyes so choose ones dense in hair....but beware the length of them! False lashes can look stupidly long once out of the packet and on the eye. Not all lashes are made equal either! If the band is too thick or stiff you'll find the lashes difficult to stick on; the ends will keep pinging up (grr!) Look for ones with a clear band which tend to be more supple. There are so many great choices out there so happy hunting!

You'll probably find they're a bit tricky to apply at first, but here are some tips to help you:

1 First check the length of the band (the bit the hairs are stuck on to) by placing along your lashline, and if it's too long (it's sticking in the corner of your eye) trim a bit off from the OUTER edge only.

2 Now apply a thin layer of glue to the band but wait for it to dry off a little first before sticking them on.

3 Look down into a mirror and use tweezers to place the lashes in the centre of the eye, then ease down the outer edge as close to the lash line as possible. Now stick down the inner edge and press lightly with your finger.

4 Once the glue has dried properly apply a little mascara at the roots to help the lashes stick to your natural lash hair for extra staying power.

#TIP

Don't try cleansing or washing mascara off your strip lashes as it ruins them! Sadly, once they get wet it's game over.

Professionally applied semi-permanent single lashes are a great solution for those with sparse lashes or for when you're on holiday. However, you can't use oily eye make-up remover (or get sun tan oil on them) as they will fall out, AND, you have to have them removed back at the salon. They're stuck onto your actual lashes with strong glue and fall out when each natural lash falls out (the cycle being about every 28 days) so they don't fall out all at once....meaning....you'll have gaps eventually which looks pretty bizarre. You can go back to the salon and get these filled in but it's a real upkeep so, if you're considering having them done, bear this in mind. It's not cheap!

LIP LINER

If you're a fan of the immaculate precision lip you'll need to invest in a lip pencil or two. Not only do they provide a guideline for your lipstick but they also help prevent bleeding.

Not ACTUAL bleeding, obvs, but the kind where your lippie travels beyond the edge of your lips and makes you look like you've been eating a jam sandwich blindfold!

Here are my few simple rules for Lipline Perfection:

ALWAYS use a liner in the exact same shade as your lipstick. The days of a dark ring around your lips are well and truly over....unless you want to channel the drag queen look, that is!

Keep your pencils sharp and if necessary, in the summer or when on hols, keep them in the fridge.

The bow of the lips looks best when they're made into two lovely rounded arches. Avoid anything too pointy looking.

Make sure you take the pencil into the very corners of the mouth to make the most of your lips.

Don't press too hard!!!! Use light strokes to define your lip shape.

You can balance out uneven lips using pencil but only to a degree, so easy does it, girlfriend. Drawing too far over your natural shape will look too fake.

Once you're happy with the line, use your ring finger to gently soften any hard edges before applying lipstick.

I always like to smudge lip liner all over the lips to create an even base for the lipstick and help intensify the lip colour.

Lip liner can be a good alternative to lipstick if you don't like the look or feel of it. Simply apply liner all over the lip, smudge in with your little finger then apply a slick of lip balm or clear gloss to give a dewy tinted look instead.

LIPSTICK

Who doesn't love a bit of lippie! Whether it's a full-on pigment rich pout or a barely-there hint of a tint – every girl's mouth should be crowned with a pop of kissable colour. I love lipstick, and what with so many different formulations available in such a fantastical array of bedazzling colours there really is something for everyone.

It's not always easy to find the shade which suits you best; it depends on your

COOL – rosy pinks, lilac pinks, lilacs, raspberry reds, blue reds, purples, pinky beiges, pinky nudes, purply plums. Avoid anything too pale or with a yellow or orange undertone but bold reds and deep strong shades can make a real statement.

WARM – coral beiges, coral nudes, peaches, corals, peachy pinks, berry pinks, oranges, orangey reds, brick reds. Warm bright shades.

OLIVE – peachy nudes, coral, rose pink, dark rose, deep apricot, orange, berries, orange reds, deep red, caramel, coffee, magenta.

DARK – browny rose, deep berries, rich plums, violets, deep reds, warm browns, magenta, purple, wine. Browny beiges make for a great nude on darker skin tones.

Right then, now you need to know some lip-trick basics:

♥ Make sure lips are smooth and kissable before applying your lipstick. Cracked flaky lips look great – said no one ever!!!

♥ You don't NEED to use a lip brush but if you want a nice sharp outline, use one!

♥ A lipstick a shade or two darker than your natural lip colour will always look good!

♥ If you can't test a lip shade on your

skin tone and hair colour which should help you decide. The general rule is that warm hair and skins look best with warm tones and cool hair and skins look best with cool tones. Warm shades have a yellow or orange undertone and cool shades have a pink or blue undertone and this rule applies to pretty much all colours (including eye shadow colours and even the colour of the clothes which will flatter you the most). A good way to tell if you're warm or cool depends how your skin behaves in the sun. If you're warm you'll tan pretty easily but if you're cool you'll burn easily, remembering that even pale skins can be warm and dark skins can be cool!. However, some people have neutral skin tones when they're actually a bit of both.....and if you're one of these lucky ladies, then you can wear any colour you like!!

Once you've established which skin tone you are you can start experimenting with lipsticks, so here's a rough guide to help you on your way:

lips test it on your fingertip not the back of your hand. Your fingertips are closer to your lip colour.

♥ Always take your natural lip colour into account; if they're pale the lipstick will look brighter but if they're dark the colour will be subdued.

♥ If you have naturally dark or blue toned lips you may have a problem with lipstick shades, especially lighter colours. Using a flesh toned pencil or a thin layer of concealer all over your lips will help neutralise the undertone so that any lip colour applied on top will be colour true.

♥ The glossier the lipstick the quicker it will wear off. Matte or satin formulations have more staying power.

♥ Dark lip colours make thin lips look even thinner. If you have thin lips but like a strong lip choose a bright punchy shade instead.

♥ Prevent lipstick from coming off on your glass by either discreetly licking your lips (or the glass) before taking a sip.

♥ If your teeth are at ALL yellow avoid all yellow undertone lip shades such as oranges or nudes which will make them look worse. Opt for bright colours preferably with a blue undertone and avoid anything metallic or chalky.

♥ When your fav lipstick wears down to the edge of the tube don't despair; you'll be amazed how much extra lipstick is hidden beneath the surface. Scoop it out and put in an empty container to use with a retractable lip brush and it'll last for ages.

LIP GLOSS

Lip gloss is the quickest and easiest way to add a bit of colour and life to your face; it's so easy you can literally apply it in the dark! There are just a handful of things I need to tell you though:

♥ Lip gloss never stays on. It's not your fault...it....just....never stays on!

♥ If lip gloss is at all sticky be careful not to rub your lips together all the time. The skin on your lips is quite delicate and the stickiness of the gloss acts like glue between the lips, pulling the skin every time you smack those kissers together.... resulting in flaking sore lips.

♥ When applying gloss over lipstick don't take it to the very edges of the lips as it will cause the lipstick to bleed and look messy.

♥ Give the illusion of fuller lips by applying just a little in the centre of the lips.

♥ Make your own lip gloss shades by mixing clear gloss with loose mineral eye shadow in pinks, golds, corals or bronzes; it can look great! You can also do this using lip balm.

♥ Clear lip gloss can look great smoothed over the eyelids for a modern wet look....but worn over coloured eye shadow it will crease. Try on a bare lid with a little long wear cream shadow underneath in your matching flesh tone.

♥ Liquid matte lipsticks are the best thing to wear under gloss if you're after the wow factor! They're not only long wearing, but create a deeply pigmented foundation for the gloss to proudly sit upon.

♥ Dazzle everyone dizzy by either dipping your gloss into a pot of glitter, or applying the glitter afterwards with a separate brush. Ker-blinggg!!

FOR HELP DECIDING WHICH PRODUCTS TO BUY, I HIGHLY RECOMMEND CHECKING OUT THIS BRILLIANT GUY; WAYNE GOSS. THERE ARE HUNDREDS OF GREAT BEAUTY BLOGGERS AND VLOGGERS OUT THERE, BUT IF IT'S ABSOLUTE HONESTY YOU'RE AFTER, WITHOUT ANY FRILLS, THEN HE'S YOUR MAN!!! HE REVIEWS JUST ABOUT EVERY NEW PRODUCT ON THE MARKET ENSURING YOU DON'T MAKE ANY COSTLY MISTAKES. BRILLIANT! @GOSSMAKEUPARTIST

JUST WING IT.
LIFE,
EYELINER,
EVERYTHING.

CHAPTER 4

IT'S ALL ABOUT
Knowledge

SHOPPING – CHOOSING CLOTHES TO SUIT YOU.

WHAT GIRL DOESN'T LOVE to shop? Well most girls actually because shopping for clothes can be one big stressful nightmare....unless you're perfectly formed, that is. But let's face it most people aren't blessed with perfectly proportioned bodies so when it comes to buying something to wear it can be the most depressing day out ever. Worry not – I have a few tips to help make these days more enjoyable and productive so you come home with bags galore and a confident skip in your step.

GENERAL TIPS

♥ Be realistic about your body shape. Don't draw attention to the bits you don't like eg. if you have a big tummy don't wear clothes which cling to your midriff. Instead wear a loose top and skinny jeans drawing attention to your legs while cleverly disguising your tum.

♥ Forget about sizing! My wardrobe is full of clothes of all different sizes; not all brands cut the same so a size 12 in one shop could be a size 10 in another or a 14 in another and yet all fit the same.

♥ Certain colours will look better on you depending on your skin tone. The darker your skin the more colours will suit you, but if you're really pale it may not be so easy. For instance, those with pinky pale skin and high colouring (prone to red flushes on the chest and cheeks) should avoid reds or cool pinks as these will only draw attention and highlight your complexion.

♥ Make sure you're wearing the right underwear when clothes shopping to give you a true representation of how you'd look if you bought the garment.

♥ When trying on clothes pick up a few sizes; I know lots of skinny models who might buy an Extra Large T-shirt or jumper for example because the slouchy look is 'in' and it looks much cooler.

♥ Check the inside label for washing instructions. If it's an item of clothing you'll wear regularly the last thing you want to see is the Dry Clean Only symbol (check out my washing chart) That silky T-Shirt

could end up costing you a lot more if it's in the cleaners every week!

♥ Charity shops can be a goldmine of cool one off pieces which nobody else will have. The best ones are in the more affluent parts of town where wealthy women can afford to continually refresh their wardrobes. Vintage clothes are brilliant too; they sometimes need a change of hemline or a nip and tuck here

and there but you can find some killer bits if you're lucky.

♥ Shoes with ankle straps can make your legs look shorter and bigger, so maybe avoid these if you have curvy calves!

♥ If you're a big girl avoid wearing horizontal stripes as they draw the eye out and make you look bigger and wider. Big patterns do the same. Look for vertical stripes and smaller prints.

♥ Don't be a slave to fashion. Every season has an array of new styles and looks so there are always choices, so though you may not be able to wear them all, some things are going to look great. For instance, I love big fluffy fake fur jackets; they look fab on Gigi Hadid and Cara Delavigne but on me? No. I look like a two-legged woolly mammoth – my boobs are too big so I just look huge and bulky.

♥ If you're short avoid big patterns as they will overwhelm you.

♥ Want to look taller? Wear plain columns of colour to elongate the body. Accessorise with long necklaces instead of short chunky ones.

♥ You have big boobs? Wearing high necks or roll-necks will make your bust look like one big shelf (voice of experience here!!) Opt for a low V neck which will be tonnes more flattering and make you look sexier too.

♥ Wear separates when shopping; if you're in a communal changing room you'll feel more confident but also, you need either a top or a bottom to give you an idea how the item would look....it's all about balance.

♥ If you're looking for a new sexy dress don't try it on with manky trainers or

scuffed boots (or even bare feet); it'll never look good. Pop a pair of heels in your bag so you can slip them on each time so you can get the full effect.

♥ If you're standing in front of the mirror 'umming' and 'aaahing' over something don't buy it; it should be instant love! That way you'll wear it loads instead of constantly trying to make it look good.

♥ Spend money on timeless wardrobe essentials such as a good black jacket which will go with everything or a pair of great fitting jeans. You can team these pieces with a cheap Tee and still look fab.

♥ Don't forget to accessorise! Jewellery, hats, scarves, belts – these things all give you an individual style and make an ordinary outfit look cooler.

♥ Layering.....always looks great. How about a slightly longer vest top under a slightly shorter top? Play with textures; a silky or lacy top peeking out below a chunky jumper looks stylish and interesting.

♥ Wear night for day! I looove a bit of a sparkle with a bit of beaten up denim.

♥ Beware the see-thru legging!! Leggings might look good on your legs, but before buying check how your bum looks as you bend down when the fabric is stretched more. We've all seen girls walking down the street looking like they've just got tights on....with their knickers blatantly on view....epic fail!

♥ Unless you're loaded don't spend lots of money on a very fashiony item; by next season it will look so out of date you won't be able to wear it again. Buy a high-street copy of the real thing instead.

♥ Different countries cut for different shapes and sizes, so certain brands clothes simply won't work on you. I've been to Japan many times but it's pointless shopping there since I'm 5'10" and absolutely nothing fits – it's all too small and too short. I don't beat myself up, I just shop elsewhere.

THE PERFECT BRA

It's essential that when you start wearing a bra you're properly measured to make sure you have the perfect fit for your individual size; we're all different and certainly when

it comes to bra's it's almost a science of its own. I still love it when I go out bra shopping and the sales girl takes one look at me (fully clothed I might add) and states my size exactly....as if she has some sort of ESP or X-Ray eyes! No – these women know their stuff and are trained to fit you to perfection. It's shocking to know as many as 80% of women wear the wrong size bra which could affect your health leading to back pain, headaches and even indigestion. Who knew!

First you need to be measured. Yes, this means a complete stranger going near your boobs but I promise you it's done on top of your clothes so there's absolutely no need to be embarrassed. These women have breasts themselves remember and they do this every day so it's no big deal at ALL. First the measuring tape is placed under your breasts OVER YOUR CLOTHES and

CHECK BEFORE BUYING WHAT THE SHOP'S RETURNS POLICY IS AND KEEP THE RECEIPT. SOME OFFER A FULL REFUND WITHIN A TIME PERIOD, AND OTHERS JUST A CREDIT NOTE SO DON'T GET CAUGHT OUT.

around your back to ascertain your back size eg. 32" or 36" etc, and then across the fullest part of the bust and around your back to ascertain the cup size eg. B, D, CC etc. The difference between the two measurements dictates the cup size! Once you know your size the sales assistant will bring you an array of bras to try. She will no doubt ask you to put the bra on then bend forward and using your hand scoop your breast into each cup... then stand up. Sounds odd, but actually this makes sure all the breast tissue is inside the cup, and then she will adjust the straps and only then decide if it's a winner or not.

WHEN CHRISTENING NEW SHOES ALWAYS CARRY A PACKET OF BLISTER PLASTERS (ORDINARY ONES WON'T WORK). THE MINUTE YOU FEEL THEM START TO RUB, GET A PLASTER ON THERE LIKE LIGHTENING BEFORE IT DEVELOPS INTO A WEEPING SEEPING SORE. WHY WEREN'T THESE INVENTED YEARS AGO; THEY'RE UNBELIEVABLY GOOD!

NEVER LEND YOUR
FAVOURITE CLOTHES
TO A FRIEND.
IF SHE RUINS THEM IT
COULD RUIN YOUR
FRIENDSHIP....SO ONLY
LEND ITEMS YOU'RE NOT
BOTHERED ABOUT!

THINGS TO REMEMBER:

♥ Get properly fitted.

♥ When bra shopping, always wear a close fitting top so you can pop it on over the bra to see what shape it gives....and if it looks lumpy, bumpy or even worse POINTY don't buy it.

♥ Your bra should not ride up your back; if it does you need a smaller size in the back.

♥ Your breasts shouldn't spill out over the edge of the cup giving a 'double boob'. This looks just awful and most unattractive...especially in a tight T-shirt. You'll need a larger cup.

♥ Your bra should give you support especially if you have big boobs; you don't want them to get saggy prematurely do you! Wearing a good bra day to day is essential and when I say 'good' I don't mean frumpy. God no! I mean well fitting.

♥ If you have large breasts you might want to avoid padded bras which will make you look bigger.

♥ Underwired bra's give the most support and will give you a different shape to a 'soft' bra.

♥ Many bras have removable padding inside which sit in a pocket inside the cup. Keeping the padding in will enhance your cleavage but beware the afore-mentioned 'D.B.' (the Double Boob!)

♥ Bra brands are like jeans brands; not every brand will suit you so don't get disheartened as they vary immensely in shape, cut, quality and style. It's trial and error I'm afraid gals.

♥ If you love sport PLEEEEAZE wear a proper sports bra or you'll live to regret it. Breasts bouncing around during exercise cause the supportive ligaments to stretch and once gone, that's it – droopy grandma boobs!

♥ Lacy bras are sexy but don't always work under certain clothes so you may want a smooth cup or a T-Shirt bra too.

♥ There is a bra for just about any style of dress. Strapless, razor back, deep plunge, backless, stick on, you name it it's out there so just ask.

♥ A plunging underwired bra will push your boobs upwards and together giving you more of a cleavage. A 'balconette' bra pushes your boobs upwards but not together, giving your breasts more of a rounded shape but not so much cleavage. Certain types of bra suit certain shapes of breasts which you'll soon see when you try on a few.

Girls get very hung up about their bodies which is such a huge shame; you might not think you're perfect, but then again who is??? It's extremely common that girls have one breast bigger than the other; this is normal. If the difference is noticeable you can always wear padding in just one cup of your bra and nobody will ever know. Sometimes one nipple is larger than the other and some girls have inverted nipples (and some men too) where the nipple doesn't stick out but all this is normal too and makes absolutely no difference when breast feeding or sexual pleasure.....so if yours are inverted or different sizes it's absolutely nothing to worry about.

BODY TAPE & SHAPEWARE

Every time we see a celeb in a low-cut plunging neckline with a fabulous cleavage it's highly likely she's using body tape. I've worked with dozens of celebrities who use it to give a gorgeous pert decolletage for those red-carpet events; you'd be surprised what goes on beneath their clothes to give the illusion of a perfect silhouette. Don't always be fooled by what you see girls. Many also love nothing more than a pair of tummy holding shapewear which hold everything in tightly and make their bottom and thighs look beautifully slim and smooth. Basically, they're no different to you; they all have their own hang ups and insecurities but use clever underwear like this to give them extra confidence.

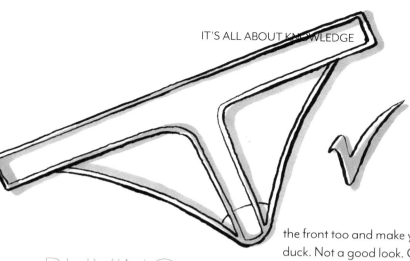

BUYING THONGS OR G-STRINGS

Nothing spoils the look more of your tight skinny jeans than an obvious VPL (Visible Panty Line). Thankfully, you have the option of wearing a Thong or G-string instead to give you a seamlessly smooth botty! However, before you grab the first pair you see you'll need to know how to spot a good one from an eye wateringly (quite literally) bad one. I am...the expert knicker picker (lol) so here's what you need to know...

First of all, spot the difference. A G-String is usually a triangle of fabric on a waistband, joined at the back by a thin strap which sits between your buttocks.... rather like a razor wire. It may as well be. G-Strings are flimsy little instruments of torture disguised as adorable pretty bits of underwear. Don't be fooled. They'll not only cut you in half at the back but

the front too and make you walk like a duck. Not a good look. Quack! Then you have what I call the 'G-String in Disguise' which looks a whole lot more comfortable but look closely....for if these have a wider piece of fabric at the back BUT a seam which goes down the middle of it...they will still have you begging for mercy... they'll still ride up and move around and generally ruin your day because the seam acts just like a string. Finally, you have the Thong which has (and this is the CRUCIAL bit) no central seam at all. The fabric at the front continues up the back and the outer edges are just neatly finished while still giving you a bump free derriere. The difference between wearing this kind and the other kinds are quite simply worlds apart; you won't even know you're wearing them and they will stay in place all day long. Sorted!

HOME ALONE - PRACTICAL SURVIVAL SKILLS AT HOME

It may well be the case that your doting mum does everything for you....lucky you! But what happens if she's out, or away, or if your mum ran off the with milkman and is no longer there to help with the practical stuff? Either way here are some handy tips to help you with some everyday hurdles...and more.

WASHING CLOTHES

You want to wear your favourite top but it's dirty and you're terrified of ruining it if you wash it yourself. Worry not!! All clothes come with a label inside which tells you how to wash and iron them and indeed if they can only be dry cleaned. So, first off, check the label. Opposite is a guide to help you decipher those strange little icons:

Machine wash

Machine wash, permanent press

Machine wash, gentle or delicate

70° Max temp 70°C or 160°F

95° Max temp 95°C or 200°F

Max temp 30°C or 80°F

bleach if needed

do not bleach

Non-chlorine bleach if needed

Hang to dry

Drip dry

Dry flat

Max temp 110°C 230°F

Max temp 150°C 300°F

Max temp 200°C 390°F

Do not dryclean

Short cycle

Reduced moisture

hand wash	do not wash	**30°** Max temp 30°C or 80°F	**40°** Max temp 40°C or 105°F	**50°** Max temp 50°C or 120°F	**60°** Max temp 60°C or 140°F
40°C or 105°F	50°C or 120°F	60°C or 140°F	70°C or 160°F	95°C or 200°F	do not wring
Non-chlorine bleach if needed	Tumble dry	Dry normal, low heat	Dry normal, medium heat	Dry normal, high heat	Dry normal, no heat
Dry in the shade	Do not dry	Do not tumble dry	Dry	Iron any temp, steam	Do not iron
No steam	Dryclean	Any solvent	Any solvent except tetrachlorethylene	Petroleum solvent only	wet cleaning
Low heat	No steam finishing				

HAND WASHING

If you can't fathom out the washing machine you can always hand wash your clothes; here's how. Half fill the sink with warm water; too cold and the dirt won't come out and too hot you may shrink the garment. Add a dose of detergent (liquid is best as doesn't need to dissolve) then place your item in the water and kind of pummel it around a bit. Any stubborn areas give them a bit of a rub. After a few minutes drain the water and rinse in cold water (lukewarm if it's wool); you may need to do this a few times until the water runs clear. Run some more water and a small measure of fabric softener... like a teaspoon as it's only one garment. Now lift out of the sink and squeeze the water out but don't wring it - you may distort the shape and ruin it. Now take a clean dry towel and lie it flat....then place the top on the towel and arrange it so it's flat too. Now roll the towel up with the top inside and when it resembles a big sausage, give it a good squeeze along the length of the roll. When you unroll the towel your top will be about 60% dry and now you just need to pop it on the radiator or put on a hanger to dry.

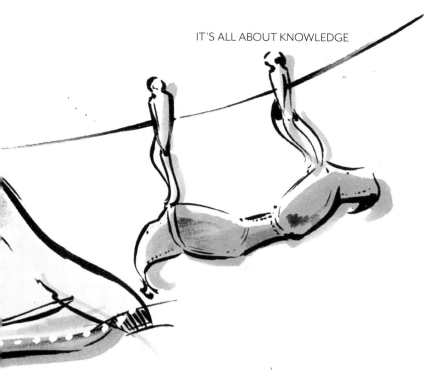

FABRIC SOFTENER should be used with care as it will, in time, rot the Lycra or elastin in your clothes and make them lose their shape. It also shouldn't always be used with towels as it affects their absorbency.

BLOOD STAINS should be treated as sooon as possible by running the fabric under COLD water; the quicker the better. Hot water can make the stain set. You can also try rubbing salt on the stain which is known to work. Follow this with a usual wash.

HOT WATER will shrink woollens so always use lukewarm water and 'delicates' detergent for these. Some machines have a 'woollens' cycle which washes at a lower temperature and spins at a lower speed so as not to stretch the fibres (landing you with a stupidly gigantic jumper)

IRONING

Many fabrics don't need to be ironed but if the thing you want to wear looks like it's been slept in you'll need a few tips:

ALWAYS keep the iron moving as you glide it over the fabric; never let it rest in one place or you'll scorch the garment leaving a cartoon shaped brown iron mark behind.

TEST the heat briefly on an unobtrusive part of the garment first to make sure the iron isn't too hot – IF it made a mark at least it'd be in an un-noticeable place.

STEAM IRONS should only be filled with distilled water or cooled water from the kettle which has been previously boiled. Water straight from the tap will cause limescale and ruin the iron.

IRONING WITHOUT STEAM is totally fine too; you simply don't put any water in the iron and don't put it on a steam setting!

NATURAL FIBRES such as cotton or linen can withstand a higher heat than manmade fibres. Check the label to see how hot the iron should be.

MANMADE FIBRES such as polyester or nylon fabrics will literally melt if the iron is too hot so make sure the iron is on a very low heat. Fabrics with Lycra don't really need ironing as they're stretchy.

MANY FABRICS have a mixture of manmade and synthetic fibres and require a medium kind of heat....but always check first.

IRONING CLOTHES INSIDE OUT is a good way of avoiding shiny seams and other minor disasters, especially when ironing silk.

WIRE HANGERS should really be thrown away as they will leave spiky lumps in the shoulders of your clothes. Once you've ironed your top, put it on a hanger that has rounded wider ends.

UNPLUG THE IRON when you're finished. Not only could it overheat and burn the house down, but the next person along might innocently pick it up and get a very nasty burn.

FOOD – THREE EASY YUMMY MEALS

If you're home alone, starving hungry, and you're not particularly handy in the cooking department you'll find these super easy, no brainer, fool-proof recipes a saviour! It's always good to have a few emergency meals up your sleeve and they can all be made from basic ingredients you probably already have in the house. Why starve or pay for an expensive (and probably unhealthy) take-away when you can rustle up one of these babies, and all with your own fair hands!

THE BEST SNACK EVER – INSTANT PIZZA!

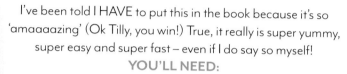

I've been told I HAVE to put this in the book because it's so 'amaaaazing' (Ok Tilly, you win!) True, it really is super yummy, super easy and super fast – even if I do say so myself!

YOU'LL NEED:

SLICED BREAD
BUTTER
TOMATO PUREE
CHEDDAR CHEESE
(mature is best if possible as it has more flavour)
DRIED MIXED HERBS
(optional)

⭐ **Place some foil in the grill pan (saves washing up later!) and put the grill on.**
⭐ **Toast the bread then butter it...but not too much**
⭐ **Spread a thick layer of tomato puree all over each slice right to the edges.**
⭐ **Cover with thick slices of cheese.**
⭐ **Season with salt and pepper to bring the flavours out and a sprinkle of mixed herbs if using.**
⭐ **Grill until the cheese bubbles and goes a bit brown.**

You can of course vary the toppings and add other things such as ham, freshly sliced tomatoes or even a few anchovies if you have some!
Deeeee-lishus!!

THE YUMMIEST SCRAMBLED EGGS EVER

Scrambled eggs, when made in a rush, are completely tasteless...and pointless. I'd rather not eat them. However, once you know the trick to perfect scrambled eggs they take on a whole new meaning of their own – you won't believe the difference I promise.

YOU'LL NEED:

3 LARGE EGGS
(per person)
SMALL KNOB OF BUTTER
SALT & PEPPER

Astonishingly, when you cook eggs slowly over a low heat they actually taste creamy, even though there's no cream in there at all. Whenever I make scrambled eggs I'm always asked if I used cream....but no....and besides my waistline is big enough thank you!!

⭐ Heat a saucepan with the knob of butter but make sure the heat is LOW!!! This is the KEY to amazing eggs.

⭐ Beat the eggs in a bowl using a fork and add a sprinkle of salt and pepper for flavour.

⭐ Pour the eggs in the pan then stir constantly with a wooden spoon. You can't walk away or run a bath or answer the phone – it's a ten minute love affair between you and the eggs so don't go wandering off!!!!

⭐ After a few minutes you'll see the texture begin to change.....keep stirring....but if the eggs start bubbling and boiling the heat is much too high so turn it right down.

⭐ Eventually the eggs will scramble but be patient; it's totally worth it. Just make sure you don't overcook them; they should be shiny and a little bit wet looking. If cooked too long the eggs will become hard and you'll lose the taste.

⭐ Serve immediately; don't let them sit in the pan because they'll keep cooking. If you're having them with toast, flick the toaster on half way through cooking the eggs so you can butter it quickly right before you dollop the eggs on top.

THE EASIEST TOMATO PASTA SAUCE EVER

Most kitchens have a bag of dried pasta hanging around, so this easy sauce will provide you with a tasty dinner with very little effort.
YOU'LL NEED:

DRIED PASTA
(spaghetti, penne, tagliatelle...
anything really!)
1 ONION –
peeled and chopped
1 CLOVE OF GARLIC,
peeled and chopped or
squished in a garlic press
LARGE TIN OF PEELED PLUM TOMATOES
or chopped tomatoes (opened and ready)
OLIVE OIL
– a splash
SALT & PEPPER
TOMATO PUREE
(don't worry if you don't have any)
Dried MIXED HERBS
(a sprinkle, optional)
KETCHUP AND VINEGAR
(optional)
CHEESE
(to serve) – fresh Parmesan is best
but grated cheddar is still absolutely fab.

FOR THE SAUCE:

☆ Heat the oil in a saucepan on a medium heat and fry the onions until they look a bit transparent and taste a bit sweet; this will take a few minutes.

☆ Add the garlic and cook for about a minute and keep stirring but watch it as garlic can easily burn and taste bitter .

☆ Chuck in the can of tomatoes, tomato puree, salt and pepper, herbs.

☆ If you have some ketchup in the fridge add a splodge, and if you have vinegar add about a teaspoon (this brings out the flavour of the tomatoes) Give it a good stir until it comes to the boil.

☆ Now turn the heat down low to a gentle simmer where the surface is bubbling but not crazily; this is how you reduce the sauce which makes it thicker and more tasty. Give it about 20 minutes.

☆ Start cooking the pasta after the sauce has been on for about ten minutes.

COOK THE PASTA LIKE THIS:

☆ Boil the kettle

☆ Fill a larger pan with the boiled water and add about a dessert spoon of salt; it looks like way too much but remember you throw the water away… and pasta cooked without salt is flavourless.

☆ Add the pasta, bring to the boil and cook for 10 to 12 mins stirring a couple of times to make sure it's not sticking together.

☆ Test if the pasta is done by running a bit under the cold tap for a second and tasting it (saves you burning your mouth!!!) It shouldn't be too hard or too soft; it should have a slight 'body' to it.

☆ Drain, give it a good shake, mix with the sauce and give it a really good stir making sure all the pasta is covered in sauce.

☆ Serve with a handful of grated cheese and devour! If you have any sauce left you could heat it up the next day and serve it with eggs, toast and bacon or halloumi cheese (grilled sliced halloumi is a scrumptious alternative to bacon y'know!)

CHAPTER 5

IT'S ALL ABOUT Love

BOYS, LOVE & RELATIONSHIPS

BOYS – HOW THEY TICK!

DO YOURSELF A FAVOUR and stop trying to fathom out how a boy thinks, because the fact is he doesn't, much. Well, he does think but not like YOU do, that's for sure. Men are simply not wired that way...the same way as us. They're a whoooole lot more straight forward and less complex so the sooner you grasp this notion the better. They don't have their hormones doing somersaults once a month so to try and compare OUR thought processes with theirs is a waste of time. While girls tell each other everything to the last detail, boys just find it pointless and boring; they'll mention you to their pals over a pint then quickly move on to who won the cup final and who scored the winning goal. It's not that they don't care, they just don't....wanna.....talk about it!

Contrary to what you believe, they don't actually inform their friends of the finer points of your body or what the two of you got up to between the sheets last night (not like girls do, by the way, we are far worse). The one thing, however, that we do have in common with the opposite sex is this; we all want to be loved. Yes, even that arrogant cock sure young buck who seems like he has a heart of stone... he wants to be loved too. The difference is that boys just don't want to show it. They want to be tough and cool, especially in front of each other, and to let their guard down and show their vulnerable side? Nope, not going to happen. A guy will only open his heart to you when he falls

> "It's not that they don't care, they just don't... wanna... talk about it"

for you....and even then he might just have to put on a show for just a bit longer in case you go off him and leave him broken hearted.....his ego in pieces, poor thing. Awww.

There are two fundamental things you need to know about boys; one is that they never actually want to hurt us, and two that often they find beautiful girls too intimidating to date. I found these nuggets of information out many years ago when sitting with a bunch of very cool and pretty hot male friends (yes, just me and a room full of HOT boys) at my old flat on Portobello Road. I asked them 'why oh why oh whyyyy' do boys lead girls on so much; why don't they just tell her if they've lost interest instead of cheating on her, leaving her in tears and making her feel like an ugly, unlovable, piece of s**t? The answer surprised me. They all agreed it was wayyy too mean to tell a girl the truth; after all they didn't want to hurt the girls feelings... 'that would be cruel' (quote, unquote) When I argued the point and said a girl would much rather the boy be honest they all recoiled in unsion, declaring I'd lost my mind – 'no waaaay' they cried – that would be awful....I think they even laughed at me. So, the next time your boyfriend acts like a complete dick, mucks you around or cheats on you it's because he's just too afraid to tell the truth (that he's lost interest) and really is pushing for YOU to dump him so that HE doesn't feel bad for hurting you.

Secondly, while on the subject of girls, I picked up a magazine and asked them who they thought was the most gorgeous. They all made different choices but they all agreed they would nevvvvvv-errrr go out with a girl that stunning – nooooooo wayyyyyy!!!! What? But why? What if a girl like that declared her undying love, surely then it would be okay? Alas no. And the reason? The reason was because a girl like that (a girl who could 'get anybody') would surely cheat on them and inevitably leave them broken hearted. None of them would be prepared to risk dating an obviously beautiful girl – how sad is that! However, what it did tell me was that boys aren't always quite as confident and self-assured as I thought, and that they, just like us, have their own insecurities (not forgetting these were cute boys too). It totally explains why there are so many lovely girls out there without boyfriends. Annoying or what!

INSIDE A BOY'S MIND

You might think you know what a guy likes but I bet you'll be surprised at some of my discoveries. Boys:

😠 DON'T like lots of makeup; most boys prefer girls to look natural. The trick is to wear make-up so that it looks natural – you gotta fool them into thinking you're naturally that pretty.

♥ DO like self-confidence. Boy's don't like insecure girls who constantly go on about their body issues; it puts them off! Even if you hate bits of yourself keep it to yourself; he wouldn't be with you if he saw you as you did.

😊 DON'T like promiscuous girls. They hate to think that half the town has seen you naked and worse still half their friends. What happens if you dump him, move on to another boy, then talk about his sexual prowess!! It may be okay for a guy to behave like this but not you, I'm afraid. This is what's known as a Double Standard; one set of rules for him and another for you. Pointless fighting it, it's just the way it is.

> "You don't need to burp the entire alphabet in his face to win his affections"

♥ DO like promiscuous girls.....but only to have a bit of naked fun with; they don't see easy girls as 'girlfriend material'.

😊 DON'T like laddish girls...not really. This is what LADS are for; to drink pints of beer with, 'F' and blind with, fart and belch with, and throw up drunk with. You don't need to burp the entire alphabet in his face to win his affections. You don't need to do this with him; it's just not.....sexy.

DO like girls who smile. Grumpy aloof sour faced girls are not attractive to boys so get your gnashers out and give him one of your finest!

DON'T like to be chased; they want to be the hunter – it makes them feel manly and once won, the prize (you) is all the sweeter. It's a basic animalistic thing so don't serve yourself on a plate; let him do most of running.

DO like to see a vulnerable side of you. He's a 'man' after all and nothing will make him feel more 'manly' than putting his big old protective arms around you and shielding you from the big bad world.

DON'T really care about your weight unless perhaps you're too far at either end of the scales (literally, which could indicate an eating disorder) Sadly most girls are obsessed with it but need to understand not all boys are attracted to the same thing. Some do like skinny girls it's true, but just about every man loves a bit of soft curvy flesh; it's super sexy.

DO like a bit of encouragement. Guys think they'll fail or be humiliated unless they get a sign form the girl they like. Sometimes a little smile or glance which lasts a moment too long will give him the green light to go ahead and approach you for a date.

DON'T like girls who don't respect themselves. If you allow him to treat you badly he'll eventually lose interest in you because you'll become less of a prize. Boys actually like, or dare I say it, NEED, to be kept on their toes. The more you let him treat you like s**t, the more he will.

DO like to have a laugh with you so let your hair down and relax...who cares if you break a nail while you play fight together.

DON'T like drunk girls. Shouty, stumbling, staggeringly drunk girls are a huge turn off for any guy.

DON'T like it when you talk in a cutesy squeaky ikkle 'Baby Voice'. They want to feel like they're with a woman, not a four-year old.

DON'T like possessiveness or jealousy; it's a sure-fire way to lose your man. If you don't trust him then why are you with him?

Boys also DON'T like too much fakery. This is a bit of a sweeping statement because some DO like girls to look really fake or 'porn star-ish' but generally speaking most boys want a girl they can take home to their mum....I KNOW it's a cliche but it's true. Generally, they don't like......

☹ Gigantic fake boobs – they don't really care what size breasts you have; they're just happy to have access to a pair, heheeee!! Girls seem to think all men like huge boobs but in fact many don't, so don't fret about yours whatever size they are.

☹ Bright orange fake tan, or treacle coloured real tan for that matter. A golden glow is far more appealing!

☹ Obvious long black cloggy fake eye lashes or eyebrows which look like they've been drawn on with a Sharpie!

> *"It might look good, but not if you want to be kissed"*

☹ Lonnnnng fake talons – scary!

☹ Gooey lip gloss – it might look great but not if you want to be kissed!

☹ Eyeliner flicks – even though girls are obsessed with a cat eye, boys quite often are not.

☹ Wedge heels - an odd one but again, I've heard it sooo many times.

☹ Lace – unless it's part of underwear it just reminds them of their granny...

especially a high-necked lace blouse; good luck with pulling in one of those!

☹ Tapestry or patchwork clothing...even if they're in fashion. Passion killers!

☹ Hairy armpits – do not embrace your inner ape ladies; leave the hairiness to him!

☹ Cheap stinky body spray or gallons of perfume everywhere! Part of the attraction between males and females of any species is smell; pheromones to be exact. They're odourless, but it's this 'smell' that rouses the senses, and if you douse yourself in anything too pongy you'll mask your natural scent. Instead, a dab of beautiful fragrance here and there is far more subtle, sexy and alluring. Pop some behind your ears, your wrists and your 'decolettage' and watch him swoon!

☹ Hair extensions – not much fun running their fingers through your hair and pulling their hand away to find it still attached.

☹ Moustaches. Always look better on a bloke. If you have one, read my advice on 'Fighting The Fuzz' and deal with it. One boy I spoke to said it was a 'deal breaker' – eek!

DOES HE LIKE ME?

Sometimes it's easy to fool ourselves that someone likes us, especially when we're attracted to them. It's easy for us to misinterpret their actions or comments into something more than they actually are, to hang on to every glance or smile or word and convince ourselves they like us. However, if a guy is truly interested in you he'll most certainly let you know. He'll call you, text you, turn up in places that you frequent and generally charm the pants off you (no pun intended) to lure you into his arms and his affections..... and bed, if he's lucky. If a guy isn't chasing you or asking you out it's because he's not interested, sorry. If you start dating a boy and he starts being flaky; not calling or being vague about seeing you, it's because he's lost interest....not his phone.

> "It's because he's lost interest, not his phone"

I've heard these imagined excuses a hundred times 'maybe his phone battery died' 'maybe he lost my number' 'maybe he fell ill' but no, I'm sorry to say there is nothing wrong with his phone, his memory, or his health. Forget him; this is a waste of your emotions, your time and your precious heart. This is going to happen a lot in your dating life and you're going to do the exact same thing to boys. I've had my fair share of heartache but I've also been the cause of it, but this is just part of learning about love, yourself, what you want and what you need. Don't ever let one rubbish boyfriend put you off dating other boys; they're not all the same and they're not the enemy. When it works it should be easy. If you're arguing all the time, break it off, find a new one. Never throw yourself away on a boy who disrespects you, ignores you, hits you, bullies you or cheats on you.

THE BIG NAUGHTY LIE

Something I simply have to share with you based on my own experiences of which there are many, is The Big Lie. Are you paying attention? Good, because you need to read this and REMEMBER this.....

When you go out on a date with a guy and he asks you back to his place he has one main objective on his mind; to get you naked. Of course, he won't tell you this, as he knows full well you'll say no. Instead he will say how much he loves your company and what a great time he's had and how the two of you can just pop back to his for 'one' last drink. He might make up an excuse that he forgot to feed the dog, water the plants, turn the oven off....whatever; he'll say

anything to lure you back into his den of seduction and before you know it you're toast! Even if you tell him 'no' because you 'know full well what will happen' he will look at you, heartbroken, wounded, and assure you with the sincerest of words and the biggest puppy dog eyes that he promises he would nev-errrr do anything like that. He'll make you feel silly for even thinking that of him. He is banking on you falling for this and if you do.....he will, 99.99999% guaranteed, try it on. He's a man, it's what they do. The times I've KICKED myself for trusting such promises and ended up in an awkward situation where I've had to extricate myself from someone's fervent grip, make for the door, infuriated at my own gullible stupidity, and annoyed that I then have to find my way home, with no idea where I am, or quite how to get back. Argh! I suppose you can't blame a guy for trying can you! So, having said that, just remember that unless you want to take things a step further, just.....don't go.

HEARTBREAK HELL – BEING DUMPED

There's a really great saying "Better to have loved and lost, than to never have loved at all". It's hard to think this way though when your heart has just been broken into a million smithereens. Your One True Love has brutally cast you aside like a dirty old sock and calmly trotted off to Happyland with Miss Bloody Perfect. It hurts! You think you'll never ever EV-ERRRRRR get over it….but you will. How do I know? Because I've been there. Several times. It's hard to imagine but when I look back there are heartbreaks I don't even remember….or at least I look back and laugh how I actually cried over that certain someone. For example, a few years ago my much younger (and less experienced) friend broke up with this guy and was really upset about it. I told her that this wimp with terrible taste in shoes (they looked like giant foot sized toffee's) and who wore way too much hair gel would soon be completely forgotten; that's she'd not only get over him but even forget he existed. Naturally she looked at me like I was some sort of lunatic, but it was only the other day I brought his name up and she said 'who?' OMG I just started wetting myself, and it was only

after I reminded her of 'the shoes' that she remembered who he was and we both fell about laughing even more. This is the nature of heartbreaks; you get over them. In fact, I can't tell you how many times this has happened; I could SHAKE myself at some of the boyfriends I've wasted my tears on…especially when I look back and realize how blinded by 'lurve' I was. So, you see if, or when (because it happens to us all), you suffer heartbreak please trust that you will get over it, you will stop crying and wailing like a toddler, you will be happy again, you will find true love and you will, most probably, forget all about your ex. It takes time to find Mr (or Mrs) right so don't let one bad experience put you off falling in love again. As I was saying, better to have loved…..

IF YOU WISH TO BE A WARRIOR PREPARE TO GET BROKEN. IF YOU WISH TO BE AN EXPLORER PREPARE TO GET LOST. IF YOU WISH TO BE A LOVER PREPARE TO BE BOTH

"Better to have loved and lost, than to never have loved at all"

DOING THE DUMPING

Don't think that just because a guy looks strong and is a 'man' that he doesn't want to be loved, or he's incapable of loving as deeply, as you do. As humans, we are all fundamentally the same in as much as we want and need to be loved.... so go easy, girls, their hearts break just as hard as ours. If you want to end a relationship be KIND; always be kind. It's just outright mean to hurt someone by saying nasty things, even if you think them, bite your lip and tell him your feelings have changed and you'd prefer to be friends instead. Put yourself in their shoes (toffee shaped or otherwise!) and imagine it's your heart that's about to be broken. Apart from that you might find that your (now) ex-boyfriend may become an invaluable friend and who knows who he's going to become friends with....if you know what I mean??? Errr.... might make some cute new friends? One step ahead ladies, one step ahead!

KISSING AND SEX – A FEW TIPS. KISSING

Starting with kissing. If you're going to be kissing someone you need to follow these few rules:

😋 DON'T eat stinky garlicky food beforehand. Don't need to elaborate here girls do I?

🖤 DO carry chewing gum with you for a quick freshen up but puh-leeease remove it beforehand. Nobody want's your half-chewed gum rattling around your mouth and potentially falling into theirs. Euch! Alternatively, a packet of mints or a mini breath freshener will do.

😊 DON'T ever kiss someone right after a cigarette; even if you don't think you smell....you do....like an ashtray..... revolting. If you smoke and the recipient doesn't, this is especially.....well it's torturous. They will never kiss you again even if you're the hottest cutest sexiest coolest girl in the world - you've blown it!

🖤 DO make sure you haven't got bits of food stuck in your teeth – not exactly enticing is it. Parsley? Anyone?

🙂 DON'T wear thick red lippy or loads of gloopy sticky lip gloss if you want to be kissed; imagine that gooey bright lip coming towards you; you'd run a mile. It's off putting.

DO relax your lips.

🙁 DON'T ram your tongue down your poor partner's throat, wiggle it around furiously or dart it in and out like a lizard.

DO make sure your lips are soft and smooth. If they resemble a cracked old potato you need to sort it out ahead of time. Brush gently with a dry toothbrush to remove any dead skin then apply lashings of lip balm. Do it the night before.

🙁 DON'T do a Moby Dick; open your mouth so wide covering all of theirs so that they think they're about to be swallowed.

DO give yourself time to learn to kiss; nobody starts out a champion kisser!

Years ago, I had a boyfriend who I loved but he just wasn't that good at kissing; it was the one small big thing. Problem! Before it got to the stage where it was too late to say anything I plucked up the courage to stop him, mid kiss, and tell him how I liked to be kissed. He didn't mind at all and became an awesome kisser. To this day he says "you taught me how to kiss!" Hell yeah!!!! What I'm saying is that when it comes to the physical side of a relationship between two people it really is a journey of discovery, and learning to be open about what you like can be great fun...providing it's put in a nice way so as not to offend anyone, eg. "I really like it when you kiss me like that, but if you kissed me like THIS I'd absolutely love it". See what I did there???

SEX

When is the right time to have sex with somebody? According to UK law it's from the age of 16 (and legally a boy could be charged with assault if you're younger) but in the actual real world where people break rules and mature at different ages, this law is often broken. The percentage of young teen pregnancies proves this! Every girl is different and some of you may wait to have sex until late into your teens or twenties, but others will experiment at a much younger age. Either way it's NOT when you feel you SHOULD be ready, or when your friends TELL you you're ready, or when your PARTNER tells you you're ready. Nope. This is YOUR body and NOBODY should make you do anything with it you don't want to do. There's no argument here; it's your choice, okay.

A short skirt is NOT a yes.

A red lip is NOT a yes.

A wink is NOT a yes.

A slow dance is NOT a yes.

A walk home is NOT a yes.

A drink back at mine is NOT a yes.

A kiss on the sofa is NOT a yes.

The only 'yes' is a 'YES'.

Sex starts out like kissing in as much as it's never good at first. I don't think I've ever met anyone who said "OMG when I lost my virginity it was like the most incredibly sexy beautiful experience of my life". It's usually more like "ugh, it was awful and awkward.....it was over quickly and I felt rather disappointed afterwards". If this is like your first experience you're not alone, but what I can say is that it gets better and better with time, maturity, and confidence.....so don't worry about it! When sex between two people is working it's just fantastic so imagine what joy lies ahead.

A few DO's and DON'T's:

DO make sure you're clean, smooth and fragrant.

DON'T drench yourself in heady perfume or nasty horrible tasting body spray.

DO wear nice underwear; sex is about ALL the senses being triggered so what your partner sees is just as much as a turn on as what they feel, taste, hear and smell. This doesn't mean black lace and rubber, by the way!

DON'T do anything you don't want to do; go as far as you want and never let anyone force you into anything you're not ready for.

DO use a condom, please. Even though it's the man who wears it there's nothing wrong with popping one in your handbag so that if he comes up with the old 'I don't have a condom on me but don't worry I'll be careful' excuse, you can ruin his day by saying "no probs hun, I've got one right here" !!!! Boys don't always like to wear a condom because it reduces sensation for them a bit, but remember it's not the boy who risks getting pregnant. He doesn't have to rock up at school or college looking like he's swallowed an ostrich, he doesn't have to go through the inevitable finger pointing and teasing, he doesn't have to go through CHILDBIRTH and if he chooses.....which some do....he can just walk away. So, for the sake of him losing an eeny weeny bit of sensation he can b****r off. Don't worry about saying "no condom, no sex, matey"

DON'T forget about STD's

DO remember that you can always change your mind. If half way through you suddenly have a change of heart (even if it's not your first time) you suddenly think 'no, don't want to', then pull away and say "I'm really sorry but I don't want to go any further, I've changed my mind". If your partner gets all narky about it let them stew; the next day they should be fine and if not, I'd seriously consider dumping them!

DON'T let anyone take photos of you in compromising positions...or naked, for that matter. In fact, unless you want to see yourself in all your butt naked glory on Instagram, Whats App, Facebook or any other social media platforms – don't do it!!!

IF YOU HAVE DOUBTS ABOUT ANYTHING SEXUAL TAKE A LOOK AT THIS WEBSITE WHO OFFER FREE HELP AND ADVICE TO YOUNG PEOPLE....AND IT'S ALL CONFIDENTIAL SO NOBODY ELSE WILL EVER KNOW! BROOK.ORG.UK

PORN

While the ideal scenario is that your parents tell you everything you need to know about sex, it's highly unlikely they'll give you any advice on how to actually do it. No parent really wants to think about their 'baby' (that's you, even though you're actually 16!!!) having S.E.X. do they. No. It's not a conversation I can imagine any parent relishing and in any case your parents, like their parents, found out by trial and error. They had to. Nobody told them so how do they know how to tell you? They didn't have the internet (no, it wasn't invented then, stop laughing!!) so it was literally 'in at the deep end' (did I really just say that???) Anyway, the internet. While it's an absolutely brilliant channel to discover all sorts of fantastic and interesting things, it's also a place where you find things which can be misleading....like porn. I'm not saying that porn is bad, but what I AM saying is that you need to understand a bit about it first before you form any ideas about sex.

Porn films are much the same as any other film in as much as the people in them are actors and they are playing a role. Ok, so in this case they're naked and the role is 'sex toy' but still there is a script, a fake set, fake relationship and the most ridiculous thing of all....fake moaning. Porn is play acting. Porn is pretend. Porn is fantasy. These people probably don't even know each other, care about each other or even fancy each other; it's just a job!!! Porn portrays the extreme in sex and by no way represents sex in a normal loving relationship. If you were to have sex with a guy dressed like a porn star, started rolling your eyes around, contorting your mouth into strange grimaces and howling like you trapped your finger in a door, you'd quite possibly get laughed at. Good or great sex doesn't rely on how many positions you can throw yourself into, and it certainly doesn't rely on you having a Barbie Doll-like body with massive breasts and a pneumatic a**e! The best sex is between two people who love each other and is far, far better than anything you'll see on film. Having threesomes, using whips and chains, handcuffing and inserting rubber things into each other or hurting each other is NOT part and parcel of everyday lovemaking. Please don't be fooled or influenced by the things you see; porn is there for entertainment not education, okay!

"Porn is play acting. Porn is pretend"

CHAPTER 6

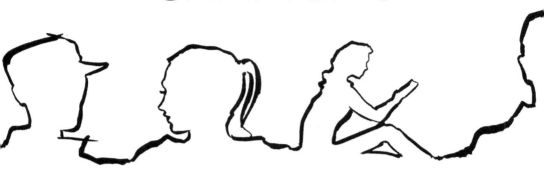

IT'S ALL ABOUT Them

PARENTS – USING THEM TO YOUR ADVANTAGE!

LIKE YOU (SORT OF) BUT OLDER!

SOMETHING YOU NEED to bear in mind is that your parents were teenagers once too. Yes, yes, they probably told you that already (YAWN) and you probably think they still wouldn't understand but hear me out. Your mum went through exactly the same stuff as you, and even though she seems to know everything now, she didn't always. Long ago she too started her periods and had to deal with that, she too wanted to be popular, beautiful, clever, have great skin and be attractive to the opposite sex....to be a grown up....to be able to smoke or drink and be cool. She hoped she would develop a great figure; have great boobs and a tiny waist and kissable lips.

Your dad also had his issues but he had a different set of them. He wanted to be popular and handsome and clever; he wanted to get the prettiest girl in school or college (so he could show off about how macho and superior he was) and to do that he needed to be great at sport, have great hair, be tall, hunky and fit, probably play the guitar but also, and this applies to every single male of the species, be well hung (because that matters a HUUUUGE great big fat deal with a man) In short, their worries and concerns, wants and needs were very much the same as yours. Your dad can help you with 'boyfriend' stuff and your mum can help you with just about everything else.

"You can't possibly, magically, know how to work it all out"

My dad always said "only a man knows how a man thinks" in the same way as only girls know how girls think, so when it comes to trying to fathom out boys...ask your dad. Anyway, going back to what I was saying, the annoying thing about being young is that you are not old; you don't have the experience of life an adult has and you can't possibly, magically, know how to work it all out.

However, what you do have is a couple of experts right under your own roof....yes.... your parents! Remember THEY ARE A MINE OF INFORMATION!!!

WHY THEY DO WHAT THEY DO

Mostly, but not in all cases, they decided to make you and therefore love you very much. Something weird but utterly natural happens when two people make a child, and when that child is born they fall completely senselessly in love with it (you, to be precise) From that moment on you become the pinnacle of all their hopes and dreams and they will do ANYTHING to protect you from the big bad world and make many, many, sacrifices along the way eg. sleep, freedom, money, time, and a little bit of sanity too (oh and did I mention saggy boobs and stretch marks?) (your mum, not your dad, obvs) Growing up you're probably rather nice; you're a child and you look to your parents for everything. You believe what they say and rely on them 100%. Then something happens.... something....quite horrid! Yes, their sweet angel turns into a dreaded TEENAGER and basically all bets are off, the rules change, and there is a divide. Them....

..Short skirt alert..

and you. The odd thing is though, that when this happens they're always still on YOUR side even if it doesn't seem that way...even if you're not on theirs. Most unfair. By now you start to question everything they say; you start to form ideas of your own. You want to spread your wings a little, push the boundaries, be independent....after all you're damned certain you know best. This is when you enter the danger zone. This is where things can go wrong but this is also where you grow....where you learn to grow up.... by getting it wrong and messing up....this is what forms you into an adult eventually. This is quite normal but you might need some guidance to get you through....

"These people will die for you, take a bullet, give you their body parts"

During this time you may start to really resent your poor old parents. You might want to shout at them and use all those forbidden words that have been festering inside, words that start with letters such as F and B and god, arrange your fingers in various shapes and thrust them in their faces. Never do this. This is not 'grown up' this is rude and pointless. When you do this, you let yourself down. You look and sound very silly. And dumb. Mostly it's hurtful and hugely disrespectful to the two people (if you have two) who love you more than anything else on planet earth. These people will die for you, take a bullet, give you their body parts – they are ON YOUR SIDE!!!!!! Always. They do not deserve your foul words and insulting hand gestures....so just....don't.

> **"YOU SPEND YEARS WISHING YOUR PARENTS WOULD GET OFF YOUR BACK, ONLY TO REALISE THEY'RE THE ONLY ONES WHO EVER REALLY HAD YOUR BACK"**

Usually you're kicking off because they're standing in the way of you and your goals such as:

⭐ Going to a party and staying out late.

⭐ Getting them to buy you stuff.

⭐ Drinking.

⭐ Smoking.

⭐ Dating older boys (remember your dad knows precisely what the boy is after even if you're adamant he doesn't. He's usually always right. Sorry to disappoint you).

⭐ Getting piercings or tattoo's in random stomach churning places.

⭐ Wearing loads of makeup, very short skirts, low cut tops or very high heels.

⭐ Borrowing their car.

...boys ahead...

...Dodgy mincab...

You get the picture right! If they're saying no it's because they're trying to protect you. They are not and I repeat NOT trying to 'ruin your life'. They're trying to prevent YOU from ruining it. Ugh, boring I know, but this is a fact. Your parents no doubt have done many of these things themselves with regrettable consequences and are merely trying to save you from a similar kind of fate. They just don't want you to:

☹ Fall under a bus, drunk.

☹ Fall under a boy (drunk).

☹ Kill yourself while driving their fast car which you're not experienced enough to handle (it's about you getting hurt, not the car, by the way).

☹ Get arrested or taken advantage of.

☹ Get accosted or fall in with the 'wrong sorts' and turn into a drug addict or alcoholic.

😞 Come home pregnant and underage...to a boy you'll never see again and therefore 'ruin your life'.

😟 Have holes, scars or pictures on your body which you may later regret and which will be either irreversible of very painful and costly to remove.

😞 They very much don't want you to 'get yourself a reputation' either (roughly translated as 'get a bad name for sleeping with way too many boys so that everyone thinks you're cheap and easy') which once lost, can never be regained.

...**Hangover ahead**...

Your parents have very vivid imaginations but infuriatingly have good reason to, but hopefully you're now starting to understand that your mum or your dad are not the enemy. You're all fighting the same war so you'll find it a lot easier to join ranks with your fellow comrades and work as a team. Just sayin'. Give them a break!

BEING A GOOD HOUSEMATE

When you're a child your parents are very happy to do absolutely everything for you, mainly because you don't know how to do stuff and hey, nobody wants a five-year old washing the bread knife do they! However, there comes a point in time when you gain full control of your limbs and your mind; arms, legs, hands and brain all working together beautifully which enables you to do all sorts of things for yourself, unaided. Freedom! (sorry, I can't resist a spot of sarcasm, heheh) Naturally you want to do all the things that YOU want to do... the fun stuff....but at some point you're going to have to start doing things you'd rather not do. Things that your parents do every day; things they don't want to do but have to do because that's just.... life. At no point did anybody ever start their day thinking "yippee, I get to take out the smelly bins, wash the dishes, clean the bath out, tidy the house, put the vacuum around, change the bedding and do piiiiles of ironing"....nope, nobody WANTS to do any of that. Nobody ever wants to walk around their home picking someone else's clothes up off the floor or find wet towels flung in a corner, along with someone else's not so fragrant underwear. Noooooo!! However, if nobody did this sort of thing you would be living in a filthy hovel. Fact. Isn't that nice that all these things are done for you! So, how about you start.....you start.... okay I'm just gonna come out and say it.... 'contributing'. Oof. Still with me? You see when you're asked to help-out, even just a bit, like tidying your room or loading the dishwasher, you're taking one job off somebody else's hands and making their day just that little bit less exhausting. You're in your teens and you want to be treated more and more like an adult; well this is the reality of being an adult. It's a mixture of doing what the hell you like (woohoo) and doing things you really don't like (meh!) So, if you want your parents to stop nagging you, the next time you're asked to help ....just....do your bit. You'll not only avoid unwanted arguments but you also gain Brownie points!!! Just follow these simple quick rules and you'll be amazed at how chilled things become.

MY 7

HOT HOUSE HACKS
FOR A HAPPIER HOME LIFE:

1 Put your wet towels back in the bathroom or on the radiator (not left in a soggy heap on the floor).

2 Replace the empty toilet roll if you're the one to finish it (major Brownie points here!!).

3 Don't leave dirty cups/plates/ glasses in your room until they go mouldy (they're a pain in the butt to clean).

4 Draw your curtains back or open your window blinds in the morning (this'll shock 'em, lol).

5 Don't leave your hair straighteners or tongs plugged in all day (best not risk burning the house down).

6 If you've had a bath, rinse it out before all those unwanted little fragments of you really stick to the tub (it's horrible for the next person to bathe).

7 If you make a snack, clean up afterwards (this includes the crumbs which are no doubt scattered everywhere!).

Now I ask you, what else can they complain about in the house? Zilch!

FRIENDS – THE SISTERHOOD

No, it's not some weird cult of incestuous nuns or a pair of matching hats; the Sisterhood is a gang you should ALL be a part of. If it wasn't for the Sisterhood I don't know where I'd be today....because my friends (the sisters I never had) have been one of the most constant things throughout my life. Guys will come and go but a true friend can be for life. I don't know how I've managed it but I've amassed quite a horde over the years (call me greedy) and the reason we're all so close is because we all believe in one thing; looking out for each other. We support and respect each other and are fiercely loyal; we'd never let a man come between us and we'd never hit on one of the others' boyfriends or husbands. We don't back-stab or bitch and we don't spread gossip or spill secrets. These are the unspoken rules of our friendships.

"If you want a friend, be a friend"

Friends should be cherished as if they were sisters but it shouldn't stop there. I believe that all us gals should stick together because really, fundamentally, we are all the same. Underneath it all, regardless of how we look or seem, we all have similar hopes and fears, we all want to find love, we all want to be beautiful and have great bodies – to be successful and popular but also we have the same insecurities and worries too....we're all fighting the same fight. So, before you judge a girl from afar or form an opinion of someone you barely know, imagine if she were you. She is somebody's daughter or sister who is loved and cherished by her family just as much as you are. Be kind. Be generous. Be united. Be a friend.

EVERYONE YOU MEET IS FIGHTING A BATTLE YOU KNOW NOTHING ABOUT. BE KIND. ALWAYS.

153

FRIENDS – AND BOYS

In a man's world, it's ok to nick your mates girlfriend or blatantly (and publicly) take the mick out of your BFF – it's seen as sport; they love it (weirdos!!!) If a bunch of girls got together and started verbally ripping each other apart or one slept with or even KISSED another girl's man, there'd be tears and resentment and the sense of betrayal and heartbreak would be immeasurable. A boy cheating on you is one thing, but a friend? Oof. If you fancy a friend's boyfriend – tough. He's out of bounds. He's off the menu. Forget it!

Flirting with your friend's boo is a massive no-no, but what if they break up....is it ok to date him? Presuming he would also like to date you and you're sure your friend is completely over him, then maybe yes....but you've got to clear it with her first. If though he has dumped her and she's broken hearted then the simple answer is no. It's not ok. It's not worth jeopardising a friendship for. I advise waiting until she's over him and got her eye on someone else, in which case you can broach it with her then and see what she says.

BITCHES & BULLIES

WHY THEY DO IT & HOW TO HANDLE IT.

Right. Let's just get one thing straight. There is absolutely no room in life for bitchiness or bullying; it is NEVER EVER acceptable and is completely and utterly wrong. I have never understood bitches or bullies and have never been one; I simply don't understand how saying mean things about someone else behind their back or openly demeaning them can be okay. It's downright cruel. A girl who behaves in this way makes herself feel better by making someone else feel bad. How pathetic is that! How can that ever be right? Why would anyone do that? Let's look at it....

BULLIES

Contrary to what you might think, mean girls aren't quite as strong or as confident as you think they are because deep down they are in fact, rather insecure and weak. They'll pick their easiest target; always someone they think won't retaliate (you'll never see a bully picking on a strong confident girl). She preys on the quiet or vulnerable because she's pretty certain she won't face any resistance....she needs a guaranteed win in order to succeed and ultimately gain a feeling of self-worth. I'm sad to say that one of my friends at school was a bit of a bully. She was beautiful, funny, very bright and had a killer figure so you'd think she'd have no reason to be nasty to anyone. However, she had an unhappy home life; her father was always out and had a string of affairs while her mother drank (probably to console herself) so I think she felt quite alone and insignificant. She was rebellious, but beneath the veneer of self-assurance and power she emitted she was clearly, and quite fundamentally, unhappy. She used to sneak off and cut her wrists.....I never knew why and she was never able to explain it; only that she felt she needed to, but it always left me feeling completely puzzled and helpless. This was my first brush with 'self-harming' and it's only now I understand what she was actually doing; it was unheard of then. Poor girl.

"I'll never forget that day; it was horrible"

This is the same girl who pushed a fellow classmate up against a wall and punched her in the face for no apparent reason...in front of everyone. I'll never forget that day; it was horrible. I think though that when you put the pieces of the jigsaw together you see the whole picture....and hopefully you see that bullies are more to be pitied than blamed; they're angry and sad and confused but the only way they can alleviate their pain is to inflict it on others (and sometimes

themselves). It's worth remembering this if you ever become the victim of one – if you can see them as weak they become a whole lot less intimidating.

DEALING WITH ONE

When I started my first secondary school, I have to say I looked like a complete square. My parents, not wanting to break the rules, kitted me out in a shiny new school uniform complete with a pair of very sensible burgundy shoes and a nice posh satchel. I had perfect shiny hair and I was in the top stream of the top form of my year; I was clever and I was tall and I was slim and the boys quite liked me. In short, I was a walking target. If there was anybody out there with a chip on their shoulder or an axe to grind, I was perfect fodder!

"I had a sudden urge to poo... she was TWICE my size!"

Enter a girl called Jackie. One day I was walking along with a friend and she strode up to me with a couple of her sidekicks and asked me if I had been dating her boyfriend.

At this point I could feel my little heart starting to beat rather fast and had a sudden urge to poo....she was TWICE my size! In fact, her boyfriend had indeed been vying for my attention but AS IF I was interested!!!!! Pipsqueak that he was! I told her 'NO!', but instead of listening to what I had to say she drew her arm back, clenched her fist and took a swing for me!! God knows how but I managed to dodge her (have you seen 'The Matrix'?) and before I knew it, by total instinct alone, I landed the most powerful right hook I could muster, right across her face, and knocked her clean to the floor. I clearly remember standing there in total disbelief as her friends, and mine, looked at me, in total shock.....Jackie laid there out cold with one cheek glowing red like a beacon! Moments later she stood up (I think I was still looking at my hand in awe as I wondered how the hell I'd done that) when she got up and stormed off with her pals....while a bunch of sixth formers cheered and clapped at the bizarre spectacle before them. The next time she saw me (after a few days of avoidance) she gave me the biggest smile and said 'Hiiiii-yaaaa' as if I was a long-lost friend. Not only did she never come near me again, but nobody in that school ever bullied me either.

I think, on reflection, she did me a favour because it taught me that a bully only has power when they have a victim, and as soon as the victim stands up to them, their power is gone. By no means am I suggesting you go around hitting people, but I'm using this story to demonstrate how easily dethroned a bully can be. A bully needs to be stopped in their tracks; you need to show them they've picked on the wrong person, even if you're scared on the inside like I was. Unless you're bullied by a Prize-fighter, the only power they have over you is their mind and their ability to intimidate, and it's your acceptance of this that they rely on.

I have one more story which I hope explains this....

I won't bore you with the details, but years later while still in my teens a situation arose regarding a boy (isn't it always) which I actually had nothing to do with but was implicated. I was told that a certain girl (who had a reputation for having anger management issues) was out to get me by way of revenge, and she had already given another girl a black eye. Apparently 'I was next'. I was scared; I knew she would never listen to me and simply annihilate me! Cut to... One day I was in a shop and she walked in. I almost had a seizure but somehow.... some....howwwww.....I mustered up the courage to approach her. She didn't have her gang there to back her up; it was just me and her in a public place.... the moment was ripe. I told her I knew she was 'looking for me' and planned to 'punch my lights out' so 'why didn't she just get on with it – now or never' I said. To be honest I was sick of watching my back and wasn't prepared to live in fear.....plus I'd calculated the risk factor of doing this

in the local sweet shop and estimated a positive outcome. I was right. She was so shocked; her face was a picture! It was the last thing she expected. She stuttered and stammered and once we'd cleared up the misunderstanding she said 'okay then' and walked away. I honestly couldn't believe it!!! And guess what....the next time I saw her...she said 'Hiiiii-yaaaa'. Funny that.

> *"She was so shocked; her face was a picture!"*

What's really important here, is that if someone is making your life miserable and it's upsetting you or getting you down, you must never just accept it or suffer alone. There's no shame in being picked on; it's not your fault – you've done nothing wrong and you don't deserve it. Fortunately, my parents taught me to stand up for myself so I wasn't afraid of confrontation (being thumped yes, but speaking up, no) but it's not an easy thing to do and for many of you it's a daunting and worrying task – even discussing it with someone you trust. However, bottling these things up isn't going to help and the stress of it will affect your wellbeing. Talk to someone. Tell your parents or a teacher....an aunt or a godparent.... and if you simply can't there are plenty of organizations you can call up or chat

to online who offer support and advice. As soon as any bullying starts it needs to be nipped in the bud, so the sooner you share this with someone the better.

There are of course those cyberbullies who don't even offer to hide who they are; they're sometimes people you know! For example, I heard about a 17 year old girl who had something really mean written about her on Facebook by a boy at school. Instead of her running off to cry in a corner she re-posted his comment to all her other school friends and said "look what this loser just sent me, in case you haven't seen it" The reaction was brilliant because everyone then posted comments on his wall telling him to quit being an a***hole and to leave the girl alone. What a fantastic way to shut someone down and shame them for their abusiveness. He obviously thought he was being clever and cool but instead he ended up openly apologising to everyone – ha!

HERE ARE JUST A COUPLE OF WEBSITES WHERE YOU CAN FIND HELP: BULLYING.CO.UK OR CHILDLINE.ORG.UK

BITCHES

Look, the same sorts of issues that drive a girl into bullying are much the same as bitching; it's all about low self-esteem. The only way to appease their sense of self-doubt, self-loathing or jealousy is by being spiteful about others, but, unlike bullying it's not so openly declared. Bitchiness is indirect aggression; the sort you don't want to get caught for and it's usually expressed whispered sneakily behind a hand. Bitches are cowards let's face it, because half the time their victim has no idea what's been said about them. It's so......pointless. I absolutely can't bear it when I'm out with a group of people and one starts slagging off another girl; it's often ones they feel threatened by too. It's easy to look at someone else and think she's perfect and it's easy to make comparisons with ourselves, but it's HIGHLY unlikely she sees herself as perfect as you see her. Who knows what thoughts go through her mind....if she hates herself, if she has problems at home, if she's suffering from an illness you know nothing about, if she feels unloved by her family......you don't know these things. Does everybody know everything about you? Do you brag about all your insecurities? No. No, you don't, and

this is why, when you're tempted with a bitchy thought or a bitchy comment, you should think twice. Be kind. By the same token the plump or spotty or unattractive girl you see being picked on or excluded from things KNOWS all these things about herself.....she doesn't need you or anybody else reminding her of her shortcomings....so again....be KIND!

HANDLING IT

So, the next time a girl says something mean about someone else what are you going to do? How about simply telling them you're not interested in bitching about people and 'can we talk about something else'. You could say 'well I like her' or 'well I think she's pretty'; say the opposite and see what reaction you get. Make fun of them for being so ridiculous. Bitches are like bullies; they need a partner in crime and without one they are a bit lost. By refusing to collaborate with a bitch you're taking away her power, saving someone from getting hurt, and you'll find others will look up to you. Being a woman in this world is hard enough and I believe we should pull together and boost each other's confidence, not destroy it. I call it THE SISTERHOOD. We have enough to cope with dealing with the opposite sex making us feel crap half the time, so let's stop raging war against our own. Stand united girls because in the end, if you don't, you'll find yourself standing alone!

"Wonder why nobody likes us...?"

give these remarks a single moment of your precious time or let them hurt you in any way. If a girl says something bitchy to you, just laugh right in her face and tell her to grow up. Get a life. Don't say mean things back....don't stoop to that level....and besides all you'll do is end up in a hideous slanging match. Tell her you couldn't give a flying 'f**k what she thinks. Look at her and say 'awwwww, is that better? Do you feel better for being mean now? Awwwww!!' and she will be so humiliated she'll never pick on you again. My mum has this great saying which I have repeated to soooo many girls because it's so true: "Better to be looked over than overlooked" – she'd say to me 'just think Jane, while they're picking on you they're leaving somebody else alone' We'd just laugh. I'm so lucky to have a mum to give me such great guidance....and happily I can share it with you.

What if you are the target of someone's bitchiness? How are you going to handle it? You've just got to laugh it off and feel sorry for them. Maybe it's easy for me to say because I quite honestly don't give a damn about what anybody thinks of me....except for my family and friends and those who I love and those who know me. Properly know me. These are the people that matter and you must approach it in the same way. You just can't let some sad petty little comments get to you; you can't

".. Hmm, Because we Hate Everybody?"

CYBER BULLIES – THE MOST COWARDLY BULLIES OF ALL!

Well I could hardly write about bullies without mentioning this bunch of tragic individuals could !? What absolute utter sh*tbags these people are; they really do make my blood boil! Anyone whose idea of a good time is sitting at a computer and being nasty to complete strangers is just....pathetic!

If a stranger is being nasty about you and posting horrible comments on any social media platform the first thing you do is report them. Report them to the site you're on as 'abusive' and block them from your feed. You must also INGORE them and NEVER enter into any dialogue with them either, because once they get a reaction, you're inviting them into your world and you won't win. A response from you will be seen as weakness, and only encourage them to sink their evil claws into you further. If you don't rise to the bait they'll soon leave you alone; if they don't score, it's game over for them. However, if they don't stop, you need to take further steps such as telling a parent or someone older who you can confide in and ask them to step in. You mustn't think 'I can handle it myself' because this sort of bullying, which can occur any hour of the day or night (unlike face to face bullying) can have a way of undermining the confidence of even the strongest person and wearing them down. It needs to be nipped in the bud ASAP so you can get on with living your life and enjoying being a fun loving young woman.

CHAPTER 7

IT'S ALL ABOUT *you*

LIKING YOURSELF

HOW YOU FEEL ABOUT YOUR LOOKS.

ONCE UPON A TIME, back in the Victorian days, it didn't matter so much how a woman looked in order to nab herself a nice husband. It mattered more that she was of good breeding stock (I think they actually used the word 'stock' as if she were a cow or a sheep......or something you made gravy with), that she had 'child bearing hips' (to help produce plenty of offspring to carry on the family name) and it would also help if she had a few social graces too such as piano playing, a pretty singing voice, or excellent embroidery skills. Imagine. I'm not sure if half the girls I meet even know how to sew a button on!

In those days beauty was nothing but a bonus but oh my, how things have changed since then. It's harder to be a woman in the world today as it's ever been, because not only are we expected to become great mothers and wives, we have to be great lovers, wonderful home-makers, brilliant business women but also we have to look bloody perfect! Seriously, this is ridiculous.

Being pretty and having a great body may seem like the be all and end all to you; the recipe to finding success and the man of your dreams, but look around you. Is every couple you see perfect or beautiful? No. By far, no! And yet, look how many couples there are....of all shapes, sizes, proportions and levels of attractiveness. They found each other didn't they....and they did it without looking like Miss World (or Mr Universe). You know why? Because while beauty is a pleasing attribute, beauty alone doesn't make you loveable. Being tall and slim with perfect breasts, a tiny waist, long leggy legs and the face of a goddess is MEANINGLESS if you're not nice on the inside. Beauty is a great calling card and of course it gets you noticed, but if it's not backed up with a good heart, a kind soul and a lovely personality you may as well look like the back end of a bus. If you're a Nasty Bitchy Moody Mean Girl, nobody is going to want to hook up with you, however stunning you are.

> **"BEAUTY CAPTURES THE EYE, BUT PERSONALITY CAPTURES THE HEART"**

SIZE MATTERS.... OR THE 'MATTER OF SIZE'

It makes me sad to say this, but over the years I've met so many girls who have eating disorders (and not all of them models, by the way). In fact, two of my closest friends have issues with their size and weight and ironically, they both happen to be gorgeous and have great figures; neither have ever been short of male attention, and in fact they get more attention when we're out than I flippin' well do. Charming! Still, it just goes to show that even those girls who we wish we looked like are just as vulnerable and lacking in confidence as we are. Argh,

why are we so damned hard on ourselves and why are we so obsessed with our weight????

I think one of the biggest problems is that we all want to look like a Victoria's Secret model…or any model…because we think that's what all guys want. If this was in fact the case, there'd be tens of thousands of single girls out there and the general population of the world would sink into rapid decline. It's an absolute cliché but BEAUTY IS IN THE EYE OF THE BEHOLDER because it all comes down to personal taste. How dull if we all looked alike. How infuriating if all guys looked the same and we only had ONE type to pick from! I have friends who think George Clooney is a GOD….but for me…. ooh noooo. You see what I'm saying? Somewhere out there is your perfect match, and when he meets you he will not belieeeeeve his luck! He will love you just the way you are, exactly as you are.

COMPARING OURSELVES

I guess we all have some star we wished we looked like (sigh!) but alas all we see when we look in the mirror is that same old face staring right back at us. But, before you start considering having a nose job, cheek implants or fillers injected into your lips, you should know exactly what goes on at a photo shoot from someone who has been on hundreds. Me.

The first thing one of these gorgeous clients usually does is apologise for the way she looks (yes really) She's probably just got off a long-haul flight in the middle of a crazy schedule and has bags under her eyes, blemished skin, lank hair and chipped nails. Thankfully she has a

You know what's really powerfully sexy? A sense of adventure. A healthy glow. Hips to grab on to. Openess. Confidence. Humility. Appeitite. Intuition… Smart-ass comebacks. Prescence. A quick wit. Dirty jokes told by an innocent looking lady… A woman who realizes how beauitful she is.

team of experts to turn her around and into the vision of herself that everybody recognizes. We go to work. The hair stylist begins their magic, usually attaching several lengths of very expensive human hair extensions to give the illusion of a glossier fuller mane. Meanwhile a manicurist is kneeling on the floor fixing and extending her nails while the make-

> "Every imperfection is masked to the max"

up artist (me again) is covering, blending, shading and highlighting her face and hiding all those things we don't want you to see. Next she goes into 'wardrobe' where a brilliant fashion stylist will put her into an outfit we could only dream of.....then, because half the time it's the wrong size, it will be pinned or stuck or sewn into place so that it looks like it fits to absolute perfection.

Underneath, by the way, there will be an artillery of body shapewear, body tape, body make-up and whatever else can be used to accentuate her every attribute. Now she's ready for the photographer.

She is now placed on a set where his (or her) assistants have spent a day or so erecting all sorts of lights and reflectors to ensure every imperfection is masked to the max. Maybe add a wind machine, and after dozens and dozens and dozens of frames being taken, the shoot is over. For her. And us. As for the photographer he/she then sends the files over to their expert re-toucher who will spend hours and hours erasing any undesirable crease, wrinkle, bulge, vein, hair, eyelash, lump bump or bruise.....before evening out and sometimes completely changing her skin tone, making her look taller and

"Maybe...they might even replace a limb"

SELF LOVE.... OR SELFIE LOVE?

thinner, whitening her teeth and the whites of her eyes.....and....maybe.....they might even replace a limb....if one looks better in another image, by the way. So, the next time you drool over a picture of a beautiful model or actress or singer remind yourself of this; even THEY wish they looked like that!!!! STOP comparing yourself – this is fakery at its finest and if you had allll that work done on you, you'd no doubt look as flawless too.

I would hate to be a teenager these days. I cannot even begin to imagine the pressure you're all under to look brilliant ALL the time and make it seem like you're having the best life ever. Posting images of yourself on social media sites daily must be utterly draining as you lie in wait for reassurance that you're 'okay'. It breaks my heart. I honestly don't know how you cope or why you do it! It's got to be soul destroying; even a celebrity couldn't cope with that kind of attention and scrutiny.

The importance placed upon how you look is out of control; it's blown out of all proportion. Love, friendships, validation – these are borne out of relationships not photographs, so please get this into perspective and give yourself a break. You don't have to be perfect and you don't have to be happy all the time; your life doesn't have to be like a blockbuster movie because in reality, NOBODY'S is. You can just be you, and that in itself, is a thing of pure beauty.

Insta sham.. I hate myself today #

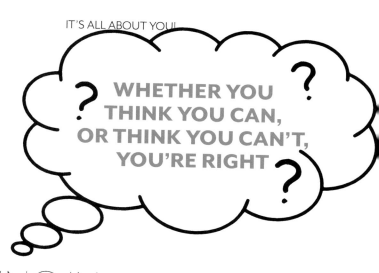

? **WHETHER YOU THINK YOU CAN, OR THINK YOU CAN'T, YOU'RE RIGHT**

BELEIVING IN YOURSELF – HOW YOU FEEL ABOUT YOU.

SELF ESTEEM

Unfortunately many people suffer from what's known as 'low self-esteem' which, simply put, is when you don't believe in yourself.....when you think you're not good enough, capable enough or worthy enough. I use the words "when you think" because it really only is 'what you think' which has nothing to do with what you actually are. It's only your opinion of you... but it doesn't mean you're right.

One of my best friends always says 'what you think about comes about' and I think she has a point! If you think you can't then you won't, but if you think you can, you open the door to all sorts of opportunities in life....so THINK POSITIVE.

Now more than ever there is so much expected of women that these nagging doubts about ourselves can stand in the way of us and finding our future happiness. You just have to try to push aside the self-doubt and dare yourself to be all that you potentially can be.... which is....anything you want to be. Have faith in yourself, don't listen to others negativity, work hard, keep focused and perhaps most of all....be brave.

"Don't let other's tales of caution or failings effect your dreams and ambitions"

CHOOSING A CAREER

I've always envied those people who know exactly what they want to do when they leave school or college; those who have a clear ambition. I wasn't one of them. When I was your age the career options for a girl were hairdresser or secretary...or housewife....none of which appealed to me!! Luckily for you, there is much more equality between the sexes now so you can do anything you darn well please.

First of all, ask yourself what you're good at....and be honest about it. It's pointless saying you want to be a world class dancer when you have two left feet! Maybe you're good at creative things like art or music, or maybe you're good with numbers and equations, cooking, writing, driving, organising things.... but remember you can't be good at everything; nobody's good at everything but everybody's good at something. Try writing it down; make a list. Now write a list of all the things you love doing, and once you've done that have a look at both lists and see if there's a marriage between what you're good at and what you enjoy. Hopefully this will give you an idea or inspiration as to what career path to follow.

So, now you've worked out what you'd like to do with your life you now need to make steps towards your goal, bearing in mind there are no short cuts! If you want a great job with a great salary you're going to have to work for it. Yep....make sacrifices too but it'll all be sooo worth it in the end. To be successful you need to put the hours in, master your craft, be patient, start from the bottom and work your way up. When I started out in make-up I was broke for a long time; I did lots and lots of jobs for nothing but I was so hungry for it I didn't mind. I was young and I was free of the responsibilities of a mortgage or children; it was all about chasing my dream and being penniless didn't matter. In time my dream began to come true and now after years of climbing up and up I can finally say 'I did it!' So, now is the time for you to begin your journey; set your goal and do everything in your power to reach it. It doesn't matter what your parents do for a living or where you come from or what other people's aspirations for you are – the only thing that matters is you and what you want. Don't let other's tales of caution or failings effect your dreams and ambitions. If you believe you can, you will.

O.C.D. – OBSESSIVE CELEBRITY DISORDER

There's such a growing obsession with 'Celebrity' and the notion that their lives are perfect, so seeing as I've spent such a lot of time with so many stars I thought I'd shed some light on the reality of what it's really like to be 'Famous'. If you think you'd be happier with your name in lights you better make sure you can handle it. Let's see.

On the up side you've probably got plenty of dosh, a big beautiful home (or two), a wardrobe to die for, a top of the range sports car, access to everywhere and anywhere you care to go and the men..... they're falling at your feet like raindrops! Doesn't it sound amazing! But is it all as glorious as it sounds? Here are just a few of the other things you'd have to cope with which aren't quite so appealing:

⭐ You must constantly look good. You can't ever be overweight, spotty or have a bad hair day and you must never ever leave the house looking less than fabulous. If not, you'll appear in about 15 weekly mags with a big red circle drawn around 'the offending area' and you'll be ridiculed by a whole host of complete strangers for....years....thanks to the internet.

⭐ You must never fall out of love with someone and in love with someone else. You'll be called a ruthless cheat and a heartbreaker.

⭐ You must never be dumped either. You'll be called 'unlucky in love' or 'a tragic figure' or they'll say you just 'can't keep your man'.

⭐ You must never eat in public. Unbeknown to you a long lens camera will mysteriously appear from a far-off bush and catch you mid bite of your favourite sarnie. You'll look like a hippo at feeding time. The whole world will see this.

⭐ Your personal life will no longer be personal! Your heartbreaks, worries and woes will be laid bare for all the world to see....along with photos of your red, tear stained puffy eyed face. Having a private life will become your biggest dream.

⭐ You must never go to the local supermarket alone....or anywhere in the Western world, for that matter. You'll be mobbed and prodded by dozens of total strangers who think it's ok to shove a camera in your face and take random pictures of you at will (theirs, not yours)

⭐ You must have the skin of a rhino...to help you cope with all the negative things which will be said about you.

⭐ You'll be constantly judged by people who you've never met and no doubt would hate if you ever did.

⭐ You must become a genius at trusting the right people. With fame comes popularity and everyone will want to be your friend. How will you know who is genuine? This goes for lovers too; how will you know if it's YOU they love or your money and success?

⭐ You have to be ok with being apart from your family and friends.....a lot. You'll be working extremely hard at all sorts of unsociable hours and travelling abroad regularly, dealing with jetlag and being knackered, and lonely, often.

You see while it may seem like Celebrities bask in a sparkly golden glow of blissfulness every day, you must remember they, like you, are only human.

"The barrage of shouting and baying paparazzi outside was so insane"

They just happen to have a job which puts them in the public eye. They have all the same sorts of feelings, doubts, insecurities and fears as you do...except the whole world knows about theirs.

Being famous in itself doesn't automatically make them happier than you or better than you. The only difference is what you do for a living. They have to make huge sacrifices to get where they are (and stay where they are) and, for all the tangible rewards they pay a huge price both psychologically, physically and emotionally. It's tough. I've worked with Celebrities for years and years and honestly don't know how they cope with all that attention....and I'm not surprised many turn to drink or drugs to help escape the craziness of it all. I remember one night going for dinner with a very famous friend, and when we left the restaurant the barrage of shouting and baying paparazzi outside was so insane we ended up going home; our evening ruined. The more I see the more I cherish being anonymous. If I want to nip out for a pint of milk in my slippers and my hair in rollers (not that I ever would – far too vain!) nobody would bat an eyelid. For a Celebrity, these simple everyday acts of freedom would soon become almost as valuable as that big house, fast car or any amount of designer clothes. Think about it.

GETTING THE BLUES – HOW YOU FEEL ABOUT LIFE

There's a word parents regularly use in conjunction with the word 'teenager' and that word is 'moody'. Well, if that doesn't put you in a mood I don't know what will – isn't it infuriating!

There's also another word used with the word 'teenage' and that word is 'angst'. Teenage angst. Looking back, I obviously had it and felt the only people who understood me were my peers – but even then, I found it hard to talk about stuff. You see, as a young child you're unaware of the harsh realities of life; the world is a lovely place where everyone is nice and the Easter bunny exists. You're free of responsibilities and your limited vocabulary doesn't even understand the meaning of words like famine, terrorism or paedophile ....or words like bereavement, heartbreak or depression. You have no idea what's in store. Enter another word: 'maturity'!

I clearly remember reaching my teenage years and feeling that I'd been duped somehow; as if I'd been conned all along, my childhood beliefs shattered. I felt as if the real villain had peeled off his smiley mask revealing his true identity, throwing his head back and cackling at my naivety. I realised that people could be mean...and hurtful...not just to me but to each other, globally....en masse. When I discovered what mankind was actually capable of, I found it utterly shocking, and I honestly struggled with the enormity of it all; I used to ask myself 'what's the point?' We are all, of course, different, but these were my personal thought processes – this was my 'angst' and yes, it made me 'moody', and sad. OBVIOUSLY, all that changed. I partly grew out of it but also adopted a more positive attitude towards things. I decided not to let the outside in, and instead focused my attentions on those I loved and my hopes and desires. I'm glad I did because it's all turned out rather damn well.

SPILL THE BEANS

Everyone has their own reason to feel miserable but you must try and get things into perspective and remember that your hormones (yes, those pesky hormones again) are largely to blame. Hormones play a huge role in our moods; just like they do when we're pre-menstrual and turn into over emotional psychopaths every month (when everything seems so much bigger than it actually is), so never underestimate how much of a part they play in your state of mind. It's normal to have feelings of sadness or depression to a degree, but so long as these feelings don't overcome you or get the better of you. If you feel like they are, then you really must share them with someone like your best friend, sibling or parent. It's a cliché but a problem shared is a problem halved; it really does take the pressure off and talking things through can really help shed a different light on things.

I don't think you should ever bottle up your feelings or feel ashamed of them; there's nothing wrong with crying - it's much the same as laughter in as much as it's completely natural...only wetter and less attractive.

BE YOUR OWN BEST FRIEND

As much as I'd love to say life is easy, the simple truth is, that it's not. Not for any of us. Sometimes it's incredibly tough but sometimes it's unbelievably magical. It's one whole big mixed bag of happiness, sadness, ups and downs, joys, trials and tribulations....it's a bit of everything thrown in together, tossed up and spat out at you randomly when you're least expecting it. It's what makes it interesting! You never know what's around the corner....or who is around the corner..... and what joys and adventures lie ahead. They say that yesterday is history, tomorrow a mystery and today is a gift... which is why it's called 'the present', so live in this moment with all the positivity you can muster. Don't dwell on things you can't change and focus on the things you can. Concentrate on making your world a better place and don't let THE world get you down. That's what I did! You're young and growing and learning and blossoming with every day; you're discovering who you are and you're definitely going to make mistakes along the way. That's how you learn, so whether you crash your parent's car for example or get drunk and make a complete arse of yourself, it's not the end of the world. Face the music, deal with it, take the

lesson with you and don't do it again. It's pointless dragging out your anguish and self-reproach. Be kind to yourself. Be your own best friend.

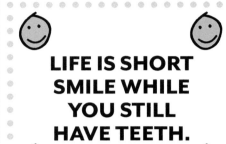

HELP YOURSELF

If you read the chapter on Panic Attacks you'll know how much just one book can make a big difference when you feel a bit lost. I'm actually not a big 'self-help book reader' as I think you can easily become overly analytical and introspective (navel gazing!). However, there are two other books which I cannot recommend more highly. The first is called 'The Seven Spiritual Laws of Success' by a brilliant man called Deepak Chopra. It's not about religion or work or law or anything like that; it's about how to be happy! I read it in my late teens and was blown away by it and fully intend to read it again

– he just puts things so simply and makes so much sense you can't believe you didn't see things that way yourself! A slightly less easy read is the second book called 'The Power of Now' by Eckhart Tolle, which teaches you how to 'live in the moment' and stop worrying about what happened in the past or what might happen in the future. If you're feeling down these books put a huge perspective on things; they're empowering and uplifting and wonderful.

Of course, there is another way to help yourself feel more positive; get some exercise! Go for a run, get some fresh air, get those endorphins going! Staying home feeling miserable (unless you're reading one of those fab books, or this one, lol) isn't going to help at all. It's a known fact that exercise enhances your mood and quite literally makes you feel better. So, what are you waiting for? Off you pop!

ALTERNATIVELY, YOU COULD CHECK OUT THIS ORGANISATION WHO OFFER GREAT ADVICE MIND.ORG.UK

HOW YOU PRESENT YOURSELF– RESPECT

When I was a teenager the only time the word 'respect' was really used was when it came to old people; 'respect the elderly' my parents would say. You'd have to let them go before you, open doors for them and give up your seat for them. Quite right – no change there then!!! When it came to 'self-respect' it was drilled into us as a matter of course so we didn't need reminding about that. However, the word 'respect' gets bandied about a whole lot more these days, but, sadly it's more often demanded then given. You're supposed to respect somebody now for no reason at all other than they're shoving their face in yours insisting upon it. It's bull***t. Respect is earned, not expected. Why on earth should someone respect you just because you think they should? And why should you respect them either?

If you want people to respect you, start by respecting yourself. Treat people how you like to be treated. Speak to people how you like to be spoken to. Behave how you like to be behaved around. Have good manners. It's simple.

MANNERS – THE LITTLE BIG THINGS WHICH MEAN A LOT!

Good manners go an awful long way in life (you'd be amazed) and if you have them, you'll be respected more..... because in having good manners you're showing respect for others and yourself. Here are my Bad Manners top 10:

Breaking wind, belching and picking your nose. It should be done in private; not to an audience and followed with an air punch of glory! You just make yourself look ridiculous, rude and unattractive. You're a GUUUURL!!!

Swearing like a rapper. Most people swear but if you replace every other word with a **** it just makes you look uneducated, attention seeking and crass. Use your brain and the rest of your vocabulary.

Eating with your mouth open or talking with your mouth full so everyone can see, and worse still hear, the food churning around your mush. Simply revolting.

Borrowing and not giving back. If your friend lends you anything; whether it be an eye liner, a jacket or a book....make sure you return it in the same condition you took it. If you lose it, replace it.

Spitting. I beg of you, don't spit on the pavement or anywhere for that matter – it's vom inducing!

Being rude to waiters. The only person it humiliates is you. NEVER do it.

Leaving your mark! When you're done in the bathroom leave it as you'd like to find it. This means no hair, toe nail clippings, toothpaste in the sink, skid marks or other body fluids in the loo. Eeew!

Don't be late. Keeping people waiting is like saying 'your time doesn't matter, you can wait for me'. It's arrogant, rude and a tad prima-donna-ish.

GOOD MANNERS OPENS CLOSED DOORS

BAD MANNERS CLOSES OPEN ONES

Talking loudly in public places. The rest of the room does not want to hear what you have to say....and if you need to answer a phone call, take it outside or into another room so everybody else doesn't have to suffer half your conversation.

Having your phone on the table when you're out at dinner, answering it if it rings, and texting. It's like inviting unwanted guests....who may have better conversation. Put your phone away or face down and on silent!

ONE LAST THING...

SO...NOW YOU'VE been advised and warned, taught and cajoled, soothed and saved and enlightened and.... dare I say it 'entertained'....I do hope you've learned even a little bit of something from my Survival Bible.

Y'know, when I was your age I had no idea how to deal with half the stuff I've talked about in this book. It's only time and experience which have taught me these things and believe me, I've made plenty of mistakes along the way. So, if you ever worry that things will never fall into place, that you'll never get things right or that you'll never get where you want to go....you WILL. Just like me. You'll get through it, you'll work it all out and soon enough you'll be on your way and chasing your dreams.

You have everything to look forward to so stay positive, believe in yourself, be kind and most of all be HAPPY! You're only here once my darlings.

ACKNOWLEDGEMENTS

My first thanks must go to Mr Hornet; the gigantic buzzing insect who took me by surprise while exiting a beautiful infinity pool in the hills of Tuscany a couple of years ago. Yes, Mr H, if you hadn't have freaked me out and caused me to turn sharply and run....I would never have torn my calf muscle, I would never have spent two months on the sofa like a stagnant potato, and I would never have made the time to write this book!

Equally importantly, I'd like to thank the wonderful teenage Tilly for begging me to do it, and for leaping down the stairs with such joy in her eyes after patiently reading through the first draft. You loved it!! Phew! I hope I've done you proud sweetheart.

Ian McDermott, my insanely talented illustrator...thank you so very much for your input, your belief in the project, your humour and your stunning imagery which has brought the pages to life. Also Graeme White, my brilliant graphic designer....thank you for being so patient, and for creating such a visually engaging little masterpiece.

Huge thanks and love to my dear friends and clients who took the time to read the TGSB and give such genuine, kind testimonials without any threat of blackmail whatsoever! Mary McCartney, Leona Lewis, Victoria Pendleton, Mary Greenwell, Holly Ramsay and Georgia Byng; you're all such fantastic role models and I'm so proud to have your names blessing my work.

Very special thanks go to my darling boyfriend Guy for your unwavering support, belief, encouragement and love. You're my rock!

Finally, eternal gratitude to my ultimate role model, my mum; the lady who taught me so many of these things and who continues to inspire me every day. Dad, I know you're looking down on me; thank you for keeping the heavens on my side and for being my ultimate hero.